ASSESSMENT TRAINING INSTITUTE
Events, Trainings and Workshops

Join ATI authors and assessment experts at one of our national workshops, or learn more about our Online and In-district Training opportunities on these topics:

Getting Started with Classroom Assessment *for* Student Learning

This one-day in-district workshop introduces K-12 educators to the two big ideas of classroom assessment quality—accuracy and the effective use of results in order to increase student motivation and learning.

🏫 On-site District Training

Leading Professional Development in Classroom Assessment *for* Student Learning

This workshop will provide the foundation needed to facilitate effective professional development in classroom assessment using a learning team model of staff development.

 Off-site Workshops

Leading Professional Development in Seven Strategies of Assessment *for* Learning

This workshop is designed to deepen understanding of how assessment *for* learning can be woven into daily teaching activities and prepare participants to lead others in their study of these practices.

Off-site Workshops

Developing Balanced Assessment Systems

This workshop takes district leadership teams though an analysis of the conditions needed for designing balanced, high-quality assessment systems. Learn how to achieve excellence in assessment that centers on three big ideas: the meaning and importance of balanced assessment, quality assessment, and assessment *for* learning.

Off-site Workshops   🖱 Online Virtual Workshop

Sound Grading Practices Conference

Presentations at this conference will provide a deeper understanding of the issues involved in sound grading practices, as well as practical strategies to change how students are graded.

Off-site Conference

Assessment Training Institute Summer Conference

Join nationally and internationally known keynote presenters at ATI's annual summer conference focused on the importance of quality assessments and assessment *for* learning.

Off-site Conference

ATI authors and consultants: Steve Chappuis, Jan Chappuis, Judy Arter and Rick Stiggins

To learn more about these training opportunities visit www.pearsonpd.com/ati

A Repair Kit for Grading

15 Fixes for Broken Grades

A Repair Kit for Grading

15 Fixes for Broken Grades

Second Edition

Ken O'Connor

Pearson Assessment Training Institute

Boston   Columbus   Indianapolis   New York   San Francisco   Upper Saddle River
Amsterdam   CapeTown   Dubai   London   Madrid   Milan   Munich   Paris   Montreal   Toronto
Delhi   Mexico City   Sao Paulo   Sydney   Hong Kong   Seoul   Singapore   Taipei   Tokyo

Vice President/Editor-in-Chief: Paul A. Smith
Editorial Assistant: Matthew Buchholz
Marketing Manager: Amanda Stedke
Production Editor: Karen Mason
Editorial Production Service: DB Publishing Services, Inc.
Manufacturing Buyer: Megan Cochran
Electronic Composition: Schneck-DePippo Graphics
Interior Design: Deb Schneck
Cover Designer: Linda Knowles
DVD Production: Picture This Production Services, Portland, Oregon

Library of Congress Cataloging-in-Publication Data

O'Connor, Ken.
  A repair kit for grading : 15 fixes for broken grades /
Ken O'Connor. — 2nd ed.
     p. cm.
  Includes bibliographical references and index.
  ISBN-13: 978-0-13-248863-1 (alk. paper)
  ISBN-10: 0-13-248863-9 (alk. paper)
  1. Grading and marking (Students) I. Title.

  LB3060.37.O273 2011
  371.27'2—dc22   2010038382

11 12 13   RRD-HA 14

www.pearsonhighered.com   ISBN-10: 0-13-248863-9
ISBN-13: 978-0-13-248863-1

Dedication

This book is dedicated to all those brave teachers who have been pioneers in grading for learning. They know who they are, and they have fixed broken grades. In this second edition I would like to acknowledge one of those brave teachers—Jane Bailey. Jane was Curriculum and Staff Development Coordinator for the Public Schools of Petoskey in Michigan. She was a dedicated educator and a delightful person who, through her writing and presenting, was a leader in the struggle for "good" grades. Sadly, Jane was diagnosed with cancer, and passed away in June 2009.

Contents

Preface

*The Committee on Grading was called upon to study grading procedures. At first, the task of investigating the literature seemed to be a rather hopeless one. **What a mass and a mess it all was!** Could order be brought out of such chaos? Could points of agreement among American educators concerning the perplexing grading problem actually be discovered? It was with considerable misgiving and trepidation that the work was finally begun.*

—W. Middleton, quoted in Guskey, 1996b, p. 13, emphasis added

This statement—or something similar—probably could have been made in almost any school or district in North America at any time in the last one hundred years. It was actually made by Warren Middleton in 1933. But it could just as easily have been said in 2010 because, although some schools and districts have forged considerable progress, grading still remains an aspect of school that is clothed in myth, mystery, and magic.

It was with equal "considerable misgiving and trepidation" that I decided to take on this difficult topic in an article for the *NASSP Bulletin* (O'Connor, 1995). That misgiving continued when I wrote *How to Grade for Learning* (O'Connor, 1999, 2002, 2009), and continues to this day.

So why a new edition, and why do I still have "misgiving and trepidation"?

This new edition is necessary because in many schools grading is still a "mass and a mess." Although teaching has become increasingly standards-based, and we know more than we ever knew about how people learn, traditional grading practices persist, especially in middle and high schools. These practices often not only result in ineffective communication about student achievement, but also may actually harm students and misrepresent their learning. Thus, I still feel the need for this "Repair Kit," in which I identify 15 ways to fix "broken" grades—15 things we should do if we want grades to be effective.

One of the major reasons for revising this book is the role of standards or learning goals (also called learning outcomes) and the increasing emphasis that the mission of schools is proficiency for *all* students. All American states now have academic content standards, as do all Canadian provinces. The mandate is that schools are supposed to be standards-based for curriculum, instruction, assessment, and grading and reporting, but what I often see, especially in middle and high schools, is some emphasis on standards for curriculum, instruction, and assessment but very little standards-based grading and reporting. My hope is that this book will help schools and teachers develop standards-based grading and reporting practices because such practices can make substantial contributions to improved student learning.

My previous book was more theoretical in its approach. This book's focus is on classroom implementation. The two books therefore complement each other, and my hope is that teachers and administrators will use them together to develop a deeper understanding of the issues in and solutions to concerns about grading. I also am pleased to report that my "misgiving and trepidation" continues to be reduced for three reasons:

1. I believe there is a growing consensus about how grades should be determined in standards-based systems (see especially Stiggins, Arter, Chappuis, & Chappuis, 2004; Tomlinson & McTighe, 2006; and Cooper, 2010 for guidelines similar to those in my works cited previously).

2. The number of districts/schools (especially high schools) that are embracing standards-based grading is steadily increasing.

3. I am also encouraged by the increasing flexibility offered in the computer grading programs that so many teachers use to determine grades.

For the bigger picture of how grading fits into classroom assessment, this book complements the books and videos produced by Rick Stiggins and his associates at Pearson's Assessment Training Institute in Portland, Oregon. The principles and ideas presented here are derived with permission from those materials, particularly Stiggins et al., 2004.

I have included examples in the text and following each Fix showing what teachers and schools use to help them implement standards-based grading and reporting and to fix broken grades, and how their use has impacted learning, learners, and teachers. I would like to thank all those who gave me permission to use these materials, but I must emphasize that they all should be seen as examples only, not as models.

My hope is that individuals and groups in schools and districts will use this book to help them to reflect on the grading practices they currently use. Each of the 15 Fixes contains quotations at the start and near the end designed to begin or focus appropriate professional dialogue.

I would like to express my appreciation to Rick Stiggins and Steve Chappuis for agreeing that there was a place for this book and for a second edition. I also thank them for the time and effort they again put into reviewing drafts of the manuscript and for their many excellent suggestions that have made it a much better book. I also would like to thank copyeditor Robert L. Marcum, project manager Denise Botelho and designer Debbie Schneck, as well as Vice President/Editor-in-Chief at Pearson Paul A. Smith, Editorial Assistant Matthew Buchholz, and Senior Production Project Editor Karen Mason for their considerable help in crafting the final product. As the author, I take full responsibility for the ideas in the book but the final product has been improved immeasurably by the contributions of those six professionals. I also express my gratitude to the thousands of teachers who have attended my workshops over the last eleven years, from whom I have learned so much.

I have made many changes in the text of this edition that hopefully make the ideas clearer and more helpful. The major changes are as follows:

- The addition of teacher vignettes and policy examples for each Fix
- A DVD video presentation in which I describe why grades are broken and discuss some of the Fixes presented in this book
- An updated learning team discussion study guide, now included at the end of the text

Ken O'Connor
Scarborough, Ontario, Canada
and The Villages, Florida
March 2010

Chapter 1

Setting the Stage

School improvement expert Bob Marzano asks, "Why [w]ould anyone want to change current grading practices? The answer is quite simple: grades are so imprecise that they are almost meaningless."

—Marzano, 2000, p. 1

Every state in the United States, every province in Canada, and almost every jurisdiction in most other countries now has educational content *standards*—public, published statements of the expected outcomes of learning; that is, what students are expected to know, understand, and be able to do. The primary goal of a standards-based system is for all students to "meet standards"; that is, to be competent or proficient in every aspect of the curriculum. The key to reaching this goal is to evaluate every student's achievement using similar criteria, consistently applied at all levels.

The two essential questions that all educators should ask about their grades are, "How confident am I that the grades students get in my classroom/school/district are accurate, meaningful, and consistent, and that they support learning?" and "How confident am I that the grades I assign students accurately reflect my school's/district's published content standards and desired learning outcomes?" In most schools/districts the answers to these questions, especially at the middle and high school levels, range from "not very" to "not at all." Because of this I believe that, very often, grades are "broken" and that teachers and schools/districts need a "repair kit." I offer such a kit here in the form of 15 Fixes that teachers and administrators alike can apply to repair broken grading systems.

Clear evidence of this broken condition can be found in the following example, from a blog on the *Washington Post* website on July 27, 2008. The previous day Jay Mathews had written an article about Matt, a student who had been asked to leave Thomas Jefferson High School of Science and Technology in Fairfax County, Virginia, because he had not attained the 3.0 GPA school policy requires that students maintain at the end of their sophomore year.

> Before I start, I would like readers to know that I am currently a rising junior at TJ (Thomas Jefferson High School for Science and Technology in Fairfax County, VA) so my views will have some bias in it (although I will do my best to minimize it). . . .

For example, I recently finished an AP chemistry course. This class was coated with extra credit, and with a 0.5 boost on GPA's, my teacher was basically handing out either a 4.0 or 4.5 for chemistry. Another AP chemistry teacher is very strict about extra credit, and rarely gives any. His course is equally challenging to my course. I got a B with extra credit, without it, I would have a C or D.

I consider myself a below par TJ student. Every class I have taken, I've always been below the class average (I even took Mrs. G. . .'s anthropology class, anyone you ask will tell you that many people take that class for the easy A. I got a B+). My current GPA is around 3.4 and *I have to admit, at least half of my sophomore grades are inflated by at least a whole letter.* If I had Matt's (the TJ student with a 2.8 GPA) combination of teachers, I would have been likely to be in his place. *The large amount of chance factors heavily on ones [sic] GPA.* (emphasis added) (zhengfranklin, 2008)

This high-stakes grading environment appears to lack consistency and accuracy, as teachers teaching the same course obviously have very different grading procedures. As Jay Mathews points out, this results in grades being *a matter of chance* as to which teacher the computer assigns a student—and this school is frequently ranked as the number one high school in the United States.

As the first "essential question" indicates, effective grades need to meet four overarching criteria for, or keys to, success: they must be accurate, meaningful, and consistent, and must support learning. I define each of these keys here and then weave them into each of the 15 Fixes throughout the rest of this book. I believe that most teachers, students, and parents would agree that these are reasonable and necessary expectations; disagreements over how to achieve them within the grade itself are at the root of the debate about grading.

First and foremost, grades need to be *accurate* reflections of student achievement. Inaccurate grades lead to poor decisions being made by and about any student whose grades are used as the basis of those decisions. When determining grades, many teachers continue the traditional practice of combining a large amount of evidence/data into a single summary symbol. This may involve literally hundreds of decisions; if even one is wrong the grade inaccurately reflects student achievement. Inaccurate grades most commonly result from teachers determining them by blending achievement with behaviors (effort, participation, adherence to class rules, etc.) (Fix 1), poor-quality assessment (Fix 10), and inappropriate use of the mean (average) in combining data (Fix 11). For grades to be "fixed," each of these practices (and others, discussed in Fixes 4, 5, 8, 9, and 12) needs to be eliminated.

Grades need to be *meaningful*. They must communicate useful information to students and to everyone interested in or needing to know about their learning. Traditionally, teachers have collected evidence using various assessment methods and have organized their gradebooks by type of evidence such as tests, projects, and assignments. So, the grading link to learning outcomes has been tentative at best. The "fix" needed for grades to be meaningful is that they must directly reflect specified learning goals. This requires that teachers set up and organize their gradebooks around those goals or standards—not simply summarize multiple marks into a single grade, or organize grades by the date administered, type of assignment or activity, or type of test—by using the standards or some organizational structure arising from or related to the standards (Fix 7). The evidence categories for mathematics, for example, may include "develops and uses number strategies," "compares and orders whole numbers to 100," and "uses estimation strategies." The evidence structure for English may use strands such as reading, writing, listening, speaking, language, and literature.

Grades need to be *consistent* across teachers. The grades students receive should not be a function of whether they are in teacher X's or teacher Y's class. The question, "How good is good enough?" needs to be the same from classroom to classroom; that is, performance standards need to be the same from teacher to teacher. Students achieving at the same level should get the same grade regardless of context. This clearly is not the case in schools where some teachers are identified as "hard" and others labeled as an "easy A," as in the example from Thomas Jefferson High School. This should *never* be acceptable. To "fix" grades, especially in standards-based systems, it is at minimum essential that all teachers in every school teaching the same grade or same subject/course should determine grades in similar ways and apply similar or the same performance standards. This consistency in the meaning of grades should be systemic at all levels—school, district, and, ideally, state/province.

Grades need to *support learning.* Students and parents need to understand that achieving in school is not only about "doing the work" or accumulating points. When teachers assign a point value to simply turning in work, or put a mark or number on everything students do and use every number when calculating the grade, the message sent to students is clear: success lies in the quantity of points earned. Any intended message about valuing the *quality* of the learning is blurred. We want students to understand that school is about learning. Grades are artifacts of learning; as such, they should reflect student achievement only (Fixes 2, 3, and 6).

Grades also support learning when the purpose of each assessment is clear. *Formative* assessments are designed to help students improve, and in almost all cases should not be used to determine grades. *Summative* assessments are designed to measure student achievement, and "are used to make statements of student learning status at a point in time to those outside the classroom" (Stiggins et al., 2004, p. 31). With some limited exceptions, only evidence from summative assessments should be used when determining grades (Fix 13). We also must allow new evidence to replace old evidence when it is clear that a student knows or can do something today that they didn't or couldn't previously (Fix 14). Finally, and perhaps most importantly, for grades to support learning, we must learn how to involve students in the grading process (Fix 15).

Key Definitions

One problem is that the terms *marks* and *grades* are often mistakenly used as synonyms, although each involves very different processes. A teacher looking at a single assessment and deciding whether a student should get 7 or 8 out of 10, or a 3 or 4 on a rubric, is doing something very different than when that teacher is looking at the evidence accumulated over a grading period and deciding whether that student gets an A or a B (or whatever summary symbols are used) on their report card. To avoid confusion, we use the following definitions throughout this book (note, however, that the sources quoted herein may not necessarily follow these definitions):

- A *mark* or *score* is the number (or letter) given to any student test or performance that may contribute to the later determination of a grade.
- A *grade* is the symbol (number or letter) reported at the end of a period of time as a summary statement of student performance.

Purpose(s) for Grades

Traditionally, grades have served a number of purposes—communication, fostering student self-assessment, sorting and selecting, motivation and punishment, and teaching/program evaluation (Guskey, 1996a). As Brookhart (2004, p. 21) points out, "It is very difficult for one measure to serve different purposes equally well." She also states, "The main difficulty driving grading issues both historically and currently is that grades are pressed to serve a variety of conflicting purposes" (p. 31). For example, for communicating effectively in a standards-driven environment where many students are succeeding, we need to be communicating the highest possible achievement in the narrowest possible range—all students are successful. However, for sorting and selecting these same students we need to spread them along the widest possible range, thus ranking some high and some low. These two purposes clearly can be in conflict. Bailey and McTighe (1996, p. 120) state that "the *primary purpose* . . . of grades [is] to *communicate student achievement* to students, parents, school administrators, post-secondary institutions and employers." Brookhart (2004, p. 5) suggests, "*Secondary purposes* for grading include providing teachers with information for instructional planning, . . . and providing teachers, administrators, parents, and students with information for selection and placement of students" (emphasis added).

A central premise of this book is that, at the district and school levels, there must be a shared vision of the primary purpose of grades. I believe that primary purpose to be communication about achievement, with *achievement* being defined as performance measured against accepted published standards and learning outcomes.

Underpinning Issues

There are three underpinning issues we must consider before addressing the specifics of how to determine grades. They are fairness, motivation, and objectivity and professional judgment.

Fairness

In education we have tended to think of *fairness* as uniformity. All students have been required to do the same assessments in the same amount of time and their grades have been calculated in the same way from the same number of assessments. But students are different in many different ways, and so treating them the same can actually be unfair. Patterson (2003, p. 572) points out that "fair does not mean equal; yet, when it comes to grading, we insist that it does." Fairness is much more about equity of opportunity than it is about uniformity. For example, some students need to wear glasses and for equity of opportunity they wear their glasses when they need them; for fairness we do not say, "You are doing a test today but you cannot wear your glasses because everyone is not wearing glasses" or "Some students in this class need glasses, so you will all wear them (whether you need them or not)."

This concept has been captured in the following statement from the policy about provincial testing in Manitoba. All teachers and jurisdictions would be serving their students well if they had a similar statement in their school/classroom assessment/grading policy:

> All students are given an equal opportunity to demonstrate what they know and can do as part of the assessment process. Adaptations . . . are *available* for students including students with learning or physical *disabilities,* to allow them to demonstrate their knowledge and skills, provided that the adaptations do not jeopardize the integrity or content of the test. (Manitoba Education, Citizenship and Youth, 2006, p. 1, emphasis added)

The italics emphasize that, for fairness, "adaptations" should not be limited to students who have been specifically identified as needing, for example, more time to complete a test/exam.

Motivation

Grades are often *extrinsic* motivators, meaning that their power to influence student behavior derives from outside the student. Many teachers—and parents, grandparents, and other adults—have used grades as extrinsic motivators ("Everyone who gets an A on this quiz can skip the next homework assignment"; "Get a B or better on that test or you can't go to the concert"). However, this use of grades is not always effective or appropriate. Grades certainly motivate successful students, at least some of the time. But they are definitely not motivators for all students, such as those who get grades that are lower than they expect or think they deserve. For these students, grades in fact often act as *de*-motivators. Many schools and school districts have mission or belief statements that state their desire to develop students who are "independent, self-directed, lifelong learners." To achieve this goal students need to be *intrinsically* motivated, meaning that their desire to achieve and improve must arise from within themselves. Intrinsic motivation is clearly in conflict with the use of grades as extrinsic motivators. Thus, as we think about our current and future grading practices, it is important that we examine and apply our knowledge and beliefs about what does and does not motivate students.

Consider this quote from Nora Rowley, the fifth-grade student who is the main character in Andrew Clements's *The Report Card*:

> Most kids never talk about it, but a lot of the time bad grades make them feel dumb, and almost all the time it's not true. And good grades make other kids think they're better, and that's not true either. And then all the kids start competing and comparing. The smart kids feel smarter and get all stuck-up, and the regular kids feel stupid and like there's no way to catch up. And the people who are supposed to help kids, the parents and the teachers, they don't. (Clements, 2004, pp. 72–73)

Clements, through Nora, makes it clear that he believes that not only do grades not motivate many students, but also that they can actually damage both student attitudes toward learning and relationships among students. Both in and out of school we provide elaborate systems of rewards and punishments in the belief that this will lead to more of those behaviors deemed desirable and less deemed undesirable. But the research on motivation shows that continued use of extrinsic motivators leads to two main results. First, extrinsic motivators increase students' focus on the reward or punishment rather than on the desired behavior. Second, they give rise to the need to continuously increase the amount of the reward or punishment to elicit the desired behavior (Covington & Manheim Teel, 1996; Gathercoal, 2004; Ginsberg, 2004; Kohn, 1993; Marshall, 2001a; Rogers, Ludington, & Graham, 1998; Szatanski & Taafe, 1999). Thus it is inappropriate to use grades as extrinsic motivators, either to reward desired behavior or to punish undesired behavior. The primary "reward" for learning should be intrinsic—the positive feelings that result from success. As Stiggins notes, "those who experience . . . success gain the confidence needed to risk trying. . . . Students who experience . . . failure, lose confidence in themselves, stop trying, and [fail] even more frequently. . . . As it turns out, *confidence is the key to student success in all learning situations*" (2001, p. 43, emphasis in original). Actual success at learning, then, is the single most important factor in (intrinsic) motivation, and it is important to recognize that success is relative—success for each individual is seeing oneself getting better.

Additionally, teachers have other tools available to help them change student behavior. As Marshall (2001b, p. 9) points out, "the most effective ways to change behaviors are: (1) using noncoercion, (2) prompting the person to self-assess, and (3) if authority is necessary, having the student own the consequence. When a consequence is imposed the student feels the victim. When the consequence is elicited, the student owns it and grows from the decision."

The best classroom practices maximize intrinsic motivation and minimize extrinsic motivation. Teachers in these classrooms help students to the critical understanding that "30 years from now, it won't matter what grades you got. What will matter is what you learned and how you used it."*

Daniel Pink (2009) writes in his recent book *Drive* that he believes that this is now also true in the world of work; the connections between motivation in the work world and in schools is examined in an interview with Pink in the May/June 2010 issue of *Edge*. He states,

> The reason to do this (emphasize intrinsic motivation) is not to be soft-hearted about it or be nicer about it. The reason to do it is because science says that if you really want high performance, particularly on those 21st century tasks, those old 19th century motivators aren't going to get you there. We need to fundamentally rethink things, not to be nicer and kinder, but to be more effective and productive. I think this approach has the ancillary benefit of being more humane, but I think it also has a very hard-headed benefit of being much more effective, much more productive, and will actually lead

---

*From a poster seen on the wall of a high school cafeteria in Council Bluffs, Iowa. Source otherwise unknown.

us to the sort of accountability that many people, including myself, think is essential. . . . The big thing is getting beyond the folklore of what really motivates people into the science of what motivates people. (Phi Delta Kappa International, 2010, pp. 5–6)

Objectivity and Professional Judgment

Teachers often say that they are striving to be as objective as possible in their assessment and grading. In my experience, they most often mean that they are trying to be *consistent* in evaluating student work. Such a process in fact involves subjective judgment. The only aspects of learning that can be assessed objectively are such elements as the correctness of factual content, spelling, and calculation.

Assessments themselves are designed subjectively. Teachers create assessments based on their professional judgment of what is to be assessed and how—a subjective process. We need to acknowledge this and not apologize. As Wiggins (2000, n.p.) notes, "All scoring by human judges, including assigning points and taking them off math homework is subjective. The question is not whether it is subjective, but whether it is defensible and credible. The Advanced Placement and International Baccalaureate assessments are subjective and yet credible and defensible, for example. So-called objective scoring is still subjective test writing." Thus the real issues are accuracy and consistency, more than objectivity versus subjectivity. We need to develop approaches to help teachers both assess and grade more accurately and consistently. One key to accomplishing this is shared understanding of performance standards— agreement on "how good is good enough?" Another is unified approaches to determining grades at the school or district level.

The problem as identified by an assistant superintendent in a Wisconsin school district is that in grading "every teacher sees himself or herself as an independent contractor and they shouldn't be" (personal communication, n.d.). What is needed is a set of guidelines such as the 15 Fixes provided in this book. Making these Fixes part of district or school policy and providing teachers frequent opportunities both for professional learning and dialogue about these guidelines and to carry out shared marking to arrive at a common understanding of performance standards will greatly enhance the probability of consistent grading across teachers and classrooms. Grading must not be a private practice; it must be a shared practice.

Student Involvement

Over the last few years it has become increasingly clear that student involvement in teaching/learning and in assessment and communication can make significant contributions to improved achievement and positive attitudes about learning/school. This issue is so significant I incorporate suggestions about it into many of the Fixes. Fix 15 is a synthesis and summary of these ideas as presented throughout the rest of the book.

The 15 Fixes

The 15 Fixes appear in Figure 1.1. They are organized into four categories—fixes for distorted achievement, fixes for low-quality or poorly organized evidence, fixes for inappropriate grade calculation, and fixes to support learning. We discuss each Fix in turn in the following chapters.

Figure 1.1 The 15 Fixes

Fixes for Practices That Distort Achievement

1. Don't include student behaviors (effort, participation, adherence to class rules, etc.) in grades; include only achievement.

2. Don't reduce marks on "work" submitted late; provide support for the learner.

3. Don't give points for extra credit or use bonus points; seek only evidence that more work has resulted in a higher level of achievement.

4. Don't punish academic dishonesty with reduced grades; apply other consequences and reassess to determine actual level of achievement.

5. Don't consider attendance in grade determination; report absences separately.

6. Don't include group scores in grades; use only individual achievement evidence.

Fixes for Low-Quality or Poorly Organized Evidence

7. Don't organize information in grading records by assessment methods or simply summarize into a single grade; organize and report evidence by standards/learning goals.

8. Don't assign grades using inappropriate or unclear performance standards; provide clear descriptions of achievement expectations.

9. Don't assign grades based on student's achievement compared to other students; compare each student's performance to preset standards.

10. Don't rely on evidence gathered using assessments that fail to meet standards of quality; rely only on quality assessments.

Fixes for Inappropriate Grade Calculation

11. Don't rely only on the mean; consider other measures of central tendency and use professional judgment.

12. Don't include zeros in grade determination when evidence is missing or as punishment; use alternatives, such as reassessing to determine real achievement, or use "I" for Incomplete or Insufficient Evidence.

Fixes to Support Learning

13. Don't use information from formative assessments and practice to determine grades; use only summative evidence.

14. Don't summarize evidence accumulated over time when learning is developmental and will grow with time and repeated opportunities; in those instances, emphasize more recent achievement.

15. Don't leave students out of the grading process. Involve students; they can—and should—play key roles in assessment and grading that promote achievement.

Chapter 2

Fixes for Practices That Distort Achievement

Fixes

1 Don't include student behaviors (effort, participation, adherence to class rules, etc.) in grades; include only achievement.

2 Don't reduce marks on "work" submitted late; provide support for the learner.

3 Don't give points for extra credit or use bonus points; seek only evidence that more work has resulted in a higher level of achievement.

4 Don't punish academic dishonesty with reduced grades; apply other consequences and reassess to determine actual level of achievement.

5 Don't consider attendance in grade determination; report absences separately.

6 Don't include group scores in grades; use only individual achievement evidence.

Fix 1

Don't include student behaviors (effort, participation, adherence to class rules, etc.) in grades; include only achievement.

Reports on student . . . achievement should contain . . . information that indicates academic progress and achievement . . . separate from . . . punctuality, attitude, behavior, effort, attendance, and work habits.
— *Manitoba Education and Training, 1997, p. 13*

*G*rades are broken when they do not accurately communicate achievement. The fix for this is to make grades as pure a measure as possible of student achievement; that is, make them reflect *only* student performance in mastering the public, published learning goals of the state/province/district/school. This is the only way that grades can act as clear communication. Everyone who has a need to know about a student's performance in school certainly can be told that she or he is "a nice student who tries hard" but they also have a right to know the specific level of her or his knowledge in a particular subject and on each standard at a given point in time.

We know that the grading practices of some teachers have contributed to grade inflation for some students by including desired behaviors unrelated to achievement, while other students who achieve at a high level have received deflated grades because of their failure to exhibit these same behaviors. For example, consider this evidence from two Canadian provinces:

16

Girls consistently outperform boys in high school classrooms across Ontario, and the explanation for the gender gap is a systematic bias against boys, the Fraser Institute says. According to six years of Grade 12 "grades" in advanced-level courses, girls get better grades more than 90% of the time in Language arts and about 60% of the time in Math. "Factors such as promptness in coming to class, willingness to cooperate, and what might be considered [good] work habits are distorting the marks," says Peter Cowley, the report's lead researcher. In other provinces where the institute's ratings have become an annual event, researchers have found girls receive better grades overall than boys even when their exam marks are lower. In B.C., "girls receive higher grades on school-based assessments in subjects regardless of their relative performance on the provincial examinations." (In British Columbia final year high school grades are determined partly from school based teacher assessment and partly from external provincial examinations.) (*Toronto* [ON] *National Post,* 18 April 2001, p. F3)

Similar evidence can be found in the United States from the Commonwealth of Virginia:

Many students . . . get passing grades by working hard in class but (their) academic weaknesses are pinpointed by the SOLs [Virginia's Standards of Learning exit tests]. (Joyce O. Jones, director of guidance at Gar-Field High School in Prince William County, VA, quoted in Helderman, 2004, p. B01)

Teachers combine achievement and other variables, such as behavior, into grades for several reasons. One is the belief that this practice appropriately rewards students who are well behaved and punishes those who do not behave as expected. When thus combined, grades become extrinsic motivators to control student behavior. As noted previously, this does not work for all students. A second reason, particularly prevalent at the high school level, is that teachers have had no way to communicate separately about the behaviors they think are important, and so have blended them together with achievement. The solution for this faulty communication is to use standards-based expanded format report cards where the desirable behaviors are listed and rated. This has become increasingly common at the elementary level, but is not yet a widespread practice in middle and high school reporting. This is somewhat ironic because at the high school level grades serve high-stakes purposes (rank in class, program and/or scholarship eligibility, college admissions, etc.) and thus should depict achievement as accurately as possible to ensure good decisions.

One of the best examples of this type of reporting is the Provincial High School report card in Ontario (www.edu.gov.on.ca/eng/document/forms/report/card/HS_Semester_First.pdf). Another excellent example is the Grade 7 and 8 report card used by the Winnipeg School Division in Manitoba (Figure 2.1). This district reports on six aspects of behavior for all students in each subject and the rubric for four levels of performance appears on the report card.

Reporting achievement separately from behaviors means that everyone can know as accurately as possible what a grade means in achievement terms. Another benefit of expanded format reporting is that it enables a school/community to show very clearly and forcefully which behaviors it values in students. Some states and many schools have articulated such statements. For example, the state of Hawaii has identified six General Learner Outcomes (GLOs) and reports on these for all students. See Figure 2.2 for an example of how teachers could record evidence for evaluating students on the basis of each GLO.

Implementing Fix 1 requires a clear statement of what behaviors and attitudes the school/district/community truly values. This will often be an extension of mission or vision statements. These valued behaviors must be published for all to see and should be revisited at least biannually for possible revision. An excellent example of clearly articulated behaviors is provided in Figure 2.3.

As you read and think about Fixes 2 through 6, keep in mind that they are subsets of the larger issue of separating behaviors from achievement. They each address specific behaviors that lead to inflated or reduced student grades, both inaccurate measures of achievement.

Figure 2.1 Winnipeg (MB) Schools Grade 7–8 Report Card

The Winnipeg School Division
Student Effort & Behaviour Report
Grade 7–8

Home Room Teacher: Student Name:
Grade: 07

KEY TO TERMS	Excellent 4	Good 3	Needs Improvement 2	Unacceptable 1
Organizational Skills	Consistently sets goals. Collects and organizes information and uses time effectively.	Usually sets goals, collects and organizes information and uses time effectively.	Frequently needs assistance in setting goals, organizing information and using time effectively.	Rarely sets goals, information disorganized and frequently wastes time.
Homework	Consistently completes homework.	Usually completes homework.	Frequently does not complete homework.	Rarely completes homework.
Assignments	Consistently brings materials and completes assignments.	Usually brings materials and completes assignments.	Frequently needs to be reminded to complete assignments.	Rarely brings materials and completes assignments.
Citizenship	Consistently respects the rights of others.	Usually respects the rights of others.	Frequently needs teacher guidance in appropriate behaviour.	Rarely demonstrates respectful behaviour.
Teamwork	Consistently participates well in class/group activities.	Usually participates well in class/group activities.	Sometimes participates well in class/group activities.	Rarely participates in class/group activities.
Interpersonal Skills	Consistently resolves conflict in constructive manner.	Usually resolves conflict in constructive manner.	Frequently needs reminder on how to resolve conflict.	Rarely resolves conflict appropriately.

ART 5 — Nixon, C

Term	1	2	3	4
Organizational Skills	3			
Homework	4			
Assignments	4			
Citizenship	3			
Teamwork	3			
Interpersonal Skills	3			

ENGLISH 7 — Palerum, U

Term	1	2	3	4
Organizational Skills	3			
Homework	3			
Assignments	3			
Citizenship	3			
Teamwork	3			
Interpersonal Skills	3			

MATH 7 — Nixon, C

Term	1	2	3	4
Organizational Skills	3			
Homework	3			
Assignments	3			
Citizenship	4			
Teamwork	4			
Interpersonal Skills	3			

MUSIC 7 — Drumstone, G

Term	1	2	3	4
Organizational Skills	3			
Homework	3			
Assignments	3			
Citizenship	3			
Teamwork	3			
Interpersonal Skills	3			

PHYS ED 7 — Pauls, T

Term	1	2	3	4
Organizational Skills	3			
Homework	3			
Assignments	3			
Citizenship	3			
Teamwork	4			
Interpersonal Skills	3			

PRACT ARTS 7 — Practical Arts Churchill

Term	1	2	3	4
Organizational Skills	3			
Homework	3			
Assignments	3			
Citizenship	3			
Teamwork	3			
Interpersonal Skills	3			

SCIENCE 7 — Nixon, C

Term	1	2	3	4
Organizational Skills	3			
Homework	3			
Assignments	3			
Citizenship	3			
Teamwork	3			
Interpersonal Skills	3			

SOCIAL STDY 7 — Pauls, T

Term	1	2	3	4
Organizational Skills	4			
Homework	4			
Assignments	4			
Citizenship	3			
Teamwork	4			
Interpersonal Skills	4			

Source: Copyright ©2002 Winnipeg School Division, Winnipeg, MB. Reprinted by permission.

Figure 2.2   State of Hawaii General Learner Outcomes
Sample Recording Sheet

Student:

Assessments → GLOs ↓				Achievement Evidence							Summary
Self-Directed Learner											
Community Contributor											
Complex Thinker											
Quality Producer											
Effective Communicator											
Effective and Ethical User of Technology											
Comments											

Note: A complete rubric for the General Learning Outcomes appears at
http://doe.k12.hi.us/standards/GLO_rubric.htm.

Student Involvement

Students benefit from frequent opportunities to identify both the
behaviors that help and those that hinder their achievement. They also
can self-assess their achievement and behaviors and set goals for both.
In furtherance of this, teachers can identify the components of desired
behaviors and help students to develop specific goals. For example, students often hear that they "need to improve their effort," but *effort* may
seem a vague concept. To help clarify this concept for students, teachers

Figure 2.3   Riffa Views International School Learner Profile

Riffa Views International School Learner Profile

The RVIS Learner Profile outlines the skills and dispositions of a RVIS student. They are derived from the school's mission and philosophy with reference to the IB Learner Profile and the Standards for the 21st Century learner.

The profile is divided into three strands. 'Skilled Learner', 'Responsible Learner' and 'Engaged Learner'. Its goal is to provide a common language and agreed upon understandings for teaching and learning about the attributes of an effective learner. Teachers, students and parents will all work together to build this shared understanding, and to reinforce these skills and dispositions with the students.

The Learner Profile plays an important role in the school's standards-based grading and reporting system. Subject grades reflect the student's achievement of the prescribed standards. The Learner Profile reflects effort, participation and behavior. Thus, students and parents receive a great deal of information about performance and about where to focus efforts to improve.

Skilled learner	Responsible learner	Engaged learner
This strand includes the core skills required for successful completion of classroom activities and assignments.	This strand is concerned with the student's capacity to meet behavioral expectations and to doing the right thing.	This strand includes the (higher order) thinking skills, habits and dispositions that predict effective, lasting learning.
• Active learner • Self-directed • Effective communicator • Organized • Collaborative • Uses feedback	• On task • Prepared • Punctual • Respectful • Caring • Fair	• Inquirer • Persistent • Shows initiative • Seeks understanding • Makes connections • Applies learning

Reprinted with permission of Riffa Views International School.

can identify the components of good effort, such as persistence, striving for accuracy, time on task, and trying alternate methods, which students then focus on to identify their relative strengths and weaknesses.

As educators, our beliefs and practices about motivation will have great impact on students. Students who have a sense of control because they know they are free to choose, and who receive frequent descriptive feedback instead of rewards and punishment linked to their behaviors, are much more likely to exhibit the desired behaviors and to value the separation of achievement and behavior.

Summary

Grades are broken when they mix achievement and nonachievement elements. The fix is to report variables such as behaviors separately from achievement, thereby ensuring that the grades reflect student achievement as accurately as possible.

> *A grade should give as clear a measure as possible of the best a student can do. Too often, grades reflect an unknown mixture of multiple factors. . . . How effective is such a communication system? The problem transcends individual teachers. Unless teachers throughout a school or district completely agree on the elements and factor them into their grading in consistent ways, the meaning of grades will vary from classroom to classroom, school to school. (Tomlinson & McTighe, 2006, p. 133)*

Teacher Vignette

Jamie Lee, Caesar Rodney School District, DE

Last year, I sat in on a parent-teacher conference regarding a male student. For all intents and purposes, the young man—I will call him Brandon— was polite and a willing worker, but not very organized. As each teacher presented Brandon's current grades and summarized his performance to his mother, I grew increasingly frustrated. Brandon was earning a "B" in my class and his science class, but failing his social studies and math classes badly. When Brandon's mother expressed her understandable concern, his social studies teacher flourished his grade printout. "You see! Brandon is clearly smart—he got a 95 percent or better on each test—but he never does his homework. I just can't pass a kid who doesn't try because it's not fair to everyone else." Brandon's math teacher offered support for the social studies teacher, noting that Brandon "never volunteers to answer problems on the board" and "never completes his homework all the way," even though Brandon was earning A's on his math tests.

To me, it was clear that Brandon was not being graded on preset academic achievement: he was being graded on his teachers' expectations of behaviors. While neither teacher questioned Brandon's academic ability, they noted that he was not on par socially with other students, and in their grading of him they allowed the grades to communicate inaccurate information about his achievement of course content.

Policy Example

Halifax Regional School Board Assessment, Evaluation and Communication of Student Learning Procedures (Revised September 24, 2008)

Policy

6.3 Grades and report cards . . . will accurately reflect achievement of the outcomes as defined by the provincial curriculum and/or individual program plan. As such, individual student achievement will . . .

> 6.3.2 Not be based on measures such as students' social development and work habits, bonus points, student absence, missed/late assignments, group scores, neatness, etc.

Procedure

Classroom Assessment

1.2 Teachers are responsible for:

> 1.2.6 Evaluating student learning by:
>
> > 1.2.6.4 Focusing on students' growth and achievements in relation to expected learning outcomes, rather than on students' characteristics and/or non-academic achievement. For example, behavior, class participation, and meeting deadlines are not curriculum outcomes and will not cause the student to gain or lose marks . . .

Don't reduce marks on "work" submitted late; provide support for the learner.

Teachers turn things in late all the time, as do workers in every profession. The idea that "You can't get away with turning work in late in the real world, mister" isn't true.

—*Wormeli, 2006, p. 148*

G rades are broken when they include penalties for student "work" submitted late. Penalties distort the achievement record the grade is intended to communicate, can actually harm student motivation, and for many students do not result in changes in behavior. The fix is to not use penalties and to set up support systems that reduce or eliminate the problem of late work.

It is critical to emphasize that we want students to exhibit responsibility and submit assessment evidence in a timely manner. The difficulty we face is, what do we do when students do not demonstrate these qualities? What policies and procedures are most likely to get them to learn as much as possible and exhibit the desired behaviors? Traditionally, we have used penalties such as a reduction of one letter grade or of a number of points for each day a required piece is late.

Many teachers believe that they need a policy with penalties to attempt to ensure that students turn in work on time so the teacher can maintain the pace of instruction necessary to meet tight curricular requirements. Many also use penalties because they believe that it communicates fairness to students: everybody gets the same amount of time. There are, however, at least four problems with this practice. First, and most damaging, they distort the grade's representation of the student's true achievement. Second, they can motivate exactly the opposite behavior than that intended. At some point in the grade reduction scenario, accumulating penalties lead students to conclude that it no longer makes sense to do that work. If it is an important piece of assessment evidence, it is better that the student submits it late than not at all. Third, my own classroom teaching experience and anecdotal evidence from many teachers leads me to conclude that penalties don't work because they do not change behavior—the same student who is late with required evidence in week 2 is frequently late in weeks 18 and 36. Fourth, having absolute deadlines (and penalties) for everything does not prepare students for the world beyond school. In the "real world" timelines are frequently negotiated (real estate, legal matters) or adjusted to circumstances (contractors and consultants); deadlines range from fixed to considerably flexible. (Ironically, "You can't deliver work late in the real world" is the very reason some teachers tell students they have the policy!) We prepare students better for that world when we offer a variety of deadlines in school; work part of an instructional sequence needs to be done tonight for tomorrow, but timelines for long-term assignments might be framed more flexibly.

Furthermore, in the world beyond school, as adults, if we are not able to meet a timeline, we often can communicate with the person/institution to whom we are responsible, arrange a new mutually agreeable timeline, and then work to meet it. This is the responsible, adult behavior that we need to encourage in students and we do this by allowing them to request extensions. This is preferable to students "hiding in the back corner" as they often do when they have late or missing assessment evidence. If we want students to be responsible and timely, then we can teach them and help them along the way, rather than assume they will learn the lessons through punitive policies.

Again, there is no suggestion here that teachers should condone or ignore lateness in submitting required evidence. Teachers should keep records of students' timeliness and report on this behavior in expanded format report cards. They also can assign consequences as they would for any other unacceptable classroom behavior. Direct parent contact may also be necessary, especially if the lateness is chronic. Students who are late with important assessment evidence could be required to come in before school, at lunchtime, or after school where they will receive both the assistance and time they need. This is similar to the approach suggested by Rick DuFour (DuFour, Eaker, DuFour, & Karhanek, 2004), whose "pyramid of interventions" to help students succeed moves from "limited and voluntary" to "significant and compulsory."

A helpful way of thinking about support and consequences was provided in a September 2008 *Educational Leadership* article, "The Teacher as Warm Demander." This concept has been put into practice as a "firm due dates" procedure at Branksome Hall, an International Baccalaureate girl's school in Toronto, Ontario, and appears in the policy example following this Fix.

The consequences for submitting required assessment evidence late should be as positive and supportive as possible, although some "negative" consequences, such as detention, may be warranted for repeated or chronic lateness. Supportive approaches do not distort achievement or motivation and more closely mirror practices in the world beyond school. Support should also include identifying at the beginning of the school year students who are organizationally challenged and providing them assistance and structure in assignments.

The most appropriate fix for grades is to not use penalties at all. Some teachers (and parents) will see the emphasis on support and communication suggested here as too "soft." Thus, as we make the transition from traditional to standards-based practices, it may be both acceptable and necessary to use small penalties that do not distort achievement or motivation; that is, penalties that are more apparent than real. One example of this approach is that students who submit required assessments late receive the grade level they "earned" but it is recorded at the lowest form of that level (e.g., a student submits an "A+" paper several days late so the grade is recorded as "A–"). The principle that should be applied to late work is to separate achievement from behavior and communicate both to those who have a right to know about the student. If Rory is a brilliant writer who always hands assignments in late, both aspects are hidden if she gets a C or a D. But if she gets an A and the report says "Brilliant writer, but always late," then we have accurate information. A daily newspaper or an advertising agency may not want to employ Rory but she may be excellent as a features writer in a monthly magazine or as a novelist or playwright.

Student Involvement

Students should have input into decisions about timelines for required assessment evidence because when they have input they have ownership, and ownership frequently leads to meeting timelines. As noted, if a student is not able to meet a timeline, the teacher should not use mark penalties, but should encourage the student to acknowledge the lateness and request an extension and/or suggest other appropriate consequences.

Summary

Penalties distort achievement and motivation, and in my experience are generally ineffective. The fix for late student work is a positive, supportive approach that directly affects student behavior, leaving the scores and the resulting grades as pure measures of achievement.

> *The appropriate consequence for failing to complete an assignment is completing the assignment. That is, students lose privileges, free time, and unstructured class or study hall time, and they are required to complete the assignment. The price of freedom is proficiency, and students are motivated not by threats of failure but by the opportunity for greater freedom and discretion when work is completed accurately and **on time**. (Reeves, 2006, p. 122, emphasis added)*

Teacher Vignette

Cindy Coffin, Assistant Superintendent of Schools with Greater Saskatoon Catholic Schools and **Cheryl Erlandson,** Director, Saskatchewan Professional Development Unit, Lecturers in the College of Education at the University of Saskatchewan

Cindy and Cheryl taught a class entitled "Classroom-Based Assessment" and took on many of the grading fixes not commonly considered in post-secondary education. The following examples discuss our practices and the effects they had on our students Brittany Boechler (teaching Grade 7/8 science at Holy Cross School in Calgary, Alberta), and Meredith Block (teaching English language arts, art, and drama at a variety of grade levels 6–12, at an American international school in South Korea).

On the two major projects in our course, due dates were provided to support planning for us and for the students. Students were told that if they submitted on or before the due dates, we would return the project by the next class and provide extensive feedback to assist students in meeting the agreed criteria. Students could revise and resubmit for reassessment any assignments up until the date of the final exam, so the due date became an incentive to gather feedback rather than a punishment if it wasn't met. We did not deduct any marks for late assignments at any time and if students were expressing difficulty understanding or achieving the criteria, we met with them either in person or by phone to support them in this. Despite not "enforcing" due dates with grades, over a four-year period, we only had one student who did not complete all assignments by the final exam.

Effect on Us

- We had positive beliefs about students and their capacity and they fulfilled those.

- We didn't have to "punish" students, but rather provided incentive for handing in work in a timely fashion.

- We felt great satisfaction as teachers in being able to work with students in meeting the criteria rather than just grading an assignment and moving on without supporting that student.

- We valued students' completion of our assignments and so used learning as the keystone rather than the timeliness of completion.

- Through this practice we demonstrated that we cared about student learning and took it seriously; consequently so did the students.

- This practice actually made the assessment process more manageable because everything didn't come in at once and we could take the time needed to provide extensive feedback.

Effect on Students

Brittany Boechler

I appreciated the flexible deadlines for assignments, as the final semester of university was an extremely busy time. Although I consider myself a hard worker, sometimes the volume of assignments could be overwhelming. The flexible deadline, along with the care and attention demonstrated by both Cheryl and Cindy, made me want to work harder and submit the highest-quality assignments that I could.

As a junior high teacher now, I give my students flexible deadlines as Cheryl and Cindy did for me. They demonstrated to me that a teacher can care and help you to succeed, even if it means simply providing you with some extra time for an assignment. My students now receive the same treatment I did, and I receive quality assignments and genuine appreciation in return.

Meredith Block

As a student, I was much more motivated to complete my tasks in a timely fashion so that I could take advantage of the opportunity to receive feedback.

- Feedback from the instructors was timely and I was able to immediately implement it in my own work; this process was particularly helpful because the feedback became something meaningful that I could work with, as opposed to a criticism of the final product with no opportunities for improvement.

- "Mistakes" and "errors" in my work became opportunities to learn and make changes, as opposed to punishments.

- I began to think of my projects as being more dynamic in nature; a work in progress, which allowed me to spend more time gathering information, reflecting on my work, and implementing necessary changes.

- Due dates became a means of organization as opposed to looming deadlines and helped to relieve some of the stress of finalizing a project.

- Knowing there would be no penalty for assignments handed in after the due date allowed me to focus on *all* of my projects in a timely fashion, and actually improved my work, because I did not feel the pressure to hand anything in until I was completely satisfied with the work.

- I felt supported and encouraged by my instructors; knowing that they genuinely cared about my learning, in turn, motivated me to work hard in class and continue to seek their counsel.

- As a teacher, I am now more concerned about ensuring that my students are able to hand in their *BEST* work, as opposed to the work they produce *on time*.

Policy Example

Branksome Hall, Toronto for Middle School and High School (MYP and DP)

4. Students are required to submit both formative and summative tasks on the due date. Practices related to supporting students in meeting deadlines include:

- Due dates are negotiated for major summative tasks/tests with the class.

- Due dates are allowed within a range of dates.

- Extensions for submission of assignments are based on individual circumstances.

- Firm due dates for major summative assessments are communicated in advance, based on reporting schedules and when work is handed back.

- Students who miss a firm due date for a summative task will be required to complete the work under the supervision of the Head of Academics and the Director of Senior School Administration. This can entail missing classes to complete the work, working in Room 101 after school or at lunch, or completing work at a supervised in-school Saturday morning work session.

- For reporting purposes, there will be firm, schoolwide cutoff dates for teachers to evaluate student work. If work is not submitted by these due dates, the report card may indicate "unable to assess" to reflect the fact that insufficient assessment data exist to make a fair evaluation of student performance of major expectations. In this case, no credit may be granted until work is submitted. Students may fail a course based on insufficient assessment evidence.

- If a student fails to submit formative or summative work on time, there will be escalating consequences:
  - The teacher must call the parents.
  - The student must attend a sitting. *(i.e., extra help session)*
  - A Missed Assignment form is completed, establishing a contract between the teacher and the student, and a copy is provided to the Guidance Counselor.
  - The student must meet with the guidance counselor to determine the source of the problem and to develop a plan to address the situation; this plan may involve required make-up work, which the student must negotiate with the teacher.
  - If a contract is broken, the student must meet with the Head of Academics and the Director of Senior School Administration, or the Assistant Head of the Middle School or the Academic Studies Coordinator.
  - A student may be withdrawn from co-curricular commitments until her work is completed.
  - For summative tasks, a student may be required to attend compulsory work sessions at a time and place determined by the Head of Academics and the Director of Senior School Administration.
  - Report card comments may include "unable to assess, work not submitted."

Fix 3

Don't give points for extra credit or use bonus points; seek only evidence that more work has resulted in a higher level of achievement.

Recently it was "Dress like an Egyptian Day" at my school. If we dressed like an Egyptian we got extra credit. When we didn't (which the majority of the kids didn't) our teacher got disappointed with us because we just "didn't make the effort." . . . One of the most frustrating things in my mind is that we get graded on something that has no educational value. I would very much like to discontinue these childish dress-up days.

—Starsinic, 2003, n.p.

Extra credit and bonus points can distort a student's record of achievement—grades are broken as a communication tool if we give points for "dressing like an Egyptian" when such "performances" do not demonstrate achievement of specified academic standards. It is obvious in the quotation that the writer, a high school senior, understands this but that her teachers do not. The fix for this is to not use extra credit or bonus points. If students want to get a higher grade teachers can require them to provide "extra" *evidence* that demonstrates a higher level of achievement.

Over the years I have heard of an amazing array of extra credit activities including cleaning blackboards, bringing in classroom supplies, supplying food for the food drive, or bringing a Mexican

32

dish for the Spanish class. My favorite story was from someone who said her high school physics teacher believed very appropriately in students identifying examples of physics in the "real world." He provided them with a "worksheet" with six questions and for each worksheet they completed 1 percent was added to their grade. Her final grade in physics was 91 percent and she did 60 extra credit sheets! It is interesting, is it not, to speculate on her level of physics knowledge? One high school science department even has an "Extra Credit Counter" (like a counter or merchandise display in a store) for each course on the school's website.

I have also heard many stories about the availability of bonus points on tests and exams so students finish with grades of 110 percent! The main problem with bonus point questions is that they are frequently conceptual or higher-order thinking questions that enable teachers to tell the difference between students who are proficient and those who are excelling. These questions should not be a matter of choice; all students should attempt them so that teachers have the evidence they need to make that critical distinction.

The basic problem with weaving extra credit and bonus points into a grade when they reflect something other than the expected learning is that they distort the record of achievement. Extra credit and bonus points stem from the belief that school is about doing the work, accumulating points, and that quantity is the key—with more being better—rather than about achieving higher levels of learning. But in standards-based systems the main issue should be having enough quality evidence to accurately determine each student's achievement. Extra credit and bonus points come from a culture that emphasizes extrinsic motivation. As with other nonachievement factors that find their way into the grade, they have frequently been used to manage student behavior.

Students should, of course, be able to provide additional evidence of their understanding, knowledge, and/or skill. However, this additional evidence must reveal new or deeper learning—and should be considered along with the previous evidence to determine the student's level of achievement. For example, if previous evidence was a mixture of the achievement levels of "competent" and "approaching competency" and a student's additional evidence was all "competent," this would allow the teacher to justify assigning this student a final achievement level of "competent" with the appropriate letter grade. (See Fix 8 for more on levels of achievement and performance standards.)

The shift in thinking is illustrated in the following example. Imagine that a student receives the following scores for a series of tests and assignments:

5/10, 66/100, 39/50, 27/35, 37/50, 8/10, 15/20, 20/25, 8/10, 75/90

The total would be 300/400, and if the grade were calculated as a mean in the traditional way the grade would be 75 percent, which in most schools/districts would be a grade of C. The student then completes three extra credit assignments (which may or may not be in any way related to the learning goals) for which he receives scores of 14/20, 7/10, and 3/5. The total is now recorded as 324/400 (although it is really 324/435) with a mean of 81 percent, so the student receives a final grade of B, which is an inflated grade.

Now imagine that a different student has a teacher who is truly standards based; this teacher records scores as proficiency levels, with 3 as proficient (meets the standard). The scores this student receives on a series of tests and assignments are 1, 2, 2, 1, 2, 2, 2, 2, 3, and 3. The mean, median, and mode for these scores are the same—2—so this student would normally receive a grade of C. The teacher, however, notes that the two more recent scores are 3s so asks the student to provide extra evidence on specific learning goals to confirm that this is now her level of achievement. The student receives 3, 4, and 3, which shows she is now proficient, so her final grade is a well-deserved B.

Student Involvement

Through self-assessment and teacher communication, students can acquire a clear sense of their level of achievement. If it is less than proficient, or lower than they (or their parents) are willing to accept, teachers can offer students opportunities to provide additional evidence. It must be clear that this will not result merely in points being added to a total. If students are able to show that they now know, understand, or can perform at a higher level, their grade must reflect this. At minimum, students should be partners in identifying appropriate evidence of additional learning, making suggestions about what they will do to show a higher level of achievement. For some it may be a traditional test, for others it will be a product, for still others it will be a performance or a personal communication such as an interview or oral exam. If they have participated appropriately in student-involved assessment they will make the right choice(s).

Summary

Grades are broken when teachers provide extra credit or bonus points that are just about more points, not about higher levels of proficiency. The fix is to eliminate extra credit and bonus points that do not relate to achievement and to communicate clearly to students and parents that better grades come from evidence of higher levels of performance, not just from more points.

> *Some teachers add "extra credit" points to the total scores. . . .*
> *This does a disservice to students when their test scores rightly*
> *show that they did not learn certain key concepts and skills and*
> *the extra credit tasks do not help the students to master those con-*
> *cepts and skills. Sometimes the extra credit work is barely, or not*
> *at all, related to the key concepts and skills that are supposed to*
> *be the basis of the grade. Not everyone agrees with my position,*
> *but I believe it is logical and fair to students. (Carr, 2000, p. 53)*

Teacher Vignette

Susan Christopher, Clayton School District, MO

I no longer give extra credit. When students approach me about wanting to improve their grade and asking for extra credit, I remind them that they have the opportunity to retake any assessment that they feel they did not do as well on as they feel they should have. The responsibility on their part is to see me for extra practice. They have to complete the extra practice before they can retake the assessment. I use the analogy of a basketball coach having a student do extra practice shooting foul shots if he/she just lost the game at the buzzer by blowing the chance at a foul shot. I also tell them that if you don't do anything differently to prepare for the assessment, you shouldn't expect the outcome to be different.

I will work with them on the extra practice or if they want to do it outside of school and give it to me, that is fine too. They just have to do something to practice. When they retake the assessment, I replace the old grade with the new grade. I do not average them.

So extra credit for me has become the opportunity to retake assessments.

Policy Examples

Minnetonka Public Schools, MN Secondary Procedures for Grading and Reporting of Pupil Achievement

1X Extra Credit

A. The purpose of extra credit is to provide additional academic work in order to enhance the learning of course standards. The following are examples of this type of extra credit:
   1. Viewing a play studied in class and writing a critical review
   2. Challenge questions at the end of a chapter review
B. The following are examples of work that **will not** count for extra credit:
   1. Nonacademic work such as bringing in materials, bathroom pass usage, merely attending extra-curricular events, signed

mid-term/permission slips, covering books, paying lab fees, and charitable donations not related to course objectives.
C.   Guidelines for application of extra credit
1. A teacher is not required to offer extra credit in any given course. Teachers of the same course will agree to any offering of extra credit.
2. In any given class in which extra credit is offered, all students in that class are eligible to earn extra credit.
4. Extra credit should encourage learning as opposed to a last-minute effort to raise a quarterly grade.

St. Michaels University School, Victoria, BC

Bonus Marks

Supplementary questions, which challenge students beyond the learning outcomes (or provide alternate routes to demonstrating mastery) are encouraged as they provide enrichment; however they will not be used as "bonus" marks. Additional "bonus" assignments or tasks provided for the purpose of "boosting" grades are not appropriate as they distort the proper assessment of a student's knowledge, skill, and understanding in relation to the learning outcomes for that course.

Fix 4

Don't punish academic dishonesty with reduced grades; apply other consequences and reassess to determine actual level of achievement.

No studies support the use of low grades or marks as punishments. Instead of prompting greater effort, low grades more often cause students to withdraw from learning.

—*Guskey & Bailey, 2001, pp. 34–35*

"You cheated, so you get a zero on this test (assignment, etc)." This has been the typical response to the discovery of academic dishonesty. It is another example of broken grades because it uses the assessment/grading policy as a tool to discipline students for inappropriate behavior, thus distorting student achievement. The fixes for this are to articulate an academic honesty policy with clear behavioral consequences for breaches and to require students to redo the test or assignment without cheating or plagiarizing, to establish an accurate achievement record for grading.

Academic dishonesty is an ongoing problem in middle and high schools and colleges. Dealing with it is often difficult; probably like many of you, I have been part of very emotional arguments about it. As with most behavioral concerns there are two main issues—how to prevent it, and what to do about it when it happens. Most schools try to deal with both of these issues together by having punitive policies that range from zeros on the assignment to loss of credit to expulsion. These policies arise from the belief that if the punishment is sufficiently severe then students will not risk being caught. Continuing academic dishonesty, however, points to the need for viable alternatives. It is perhaps best to begin with how to prevent it, then develop procedures to deal with it when it happens.

"Prevention is better than cure" is an old but true saying, and it certainly applies here. Tom Solyom, when he was an assistant principal, and teacher-librarian Dawn Keer at Archbishop Macdonald High School in Edmonton, Alberta, led the development of a policy aimed at decreasing cheating. They believe that teachers must make their expectations clear and explicit and should talk about academic integrity with their students to help them understand why it is so important. They also believe that teachers should not assume that students understand exactly what they mean by the terms *plagiarism* or *cheating*.

The policy statement at the school provides the following "Definitions of Inappropriate Academic Behavior/Academic Misconduct":

Plagiarism
Submitting the words, ideas, images or data of another person's as one's own in any academic writing or other project.

Cheating
a) Possession of unauthorized material,
b) Substantial editorial or compositional assistance,
c) Submission of another student's material already graded for credit,
d) False claims or fabricated references,
e) Copying off of someone else's exam and/or quiz; or passing answers from a quiz or exam to another student.
(Archbishop Macdonald High School, 2006, p. 27)

The faculty was also provided with a list of "Tips for Preventing Plagiarism and Cheating," which appear on the next page (remember, it is a high school!).

1. Assign essay topics that are specific to your course and timely in nature.

2. Give clear guidelines for format.

3. Provide bibliography resources. (Websites, guidebooks, etc.)

4. Give your class an example of a plagiarized paper and have a discussion about it.

5. Use in-class writing assignments.

6. Set assignments where the objective is to critique websites, thus avoiding the temptation for students to copy them.

7. Change your exams every term and/or use alternating formats so students next to each other are not writing identical exams.

8. Proctor your exams. During mid-term and final exams, make sure there are enough supervisors (proctors) for the number of students.

9. Where possible arrange students with a seat in between them. (This is obviously difficult with large classes.)

10. Provide scratch paper.

11. Whenever possible, use long answer/essay format. (Math could have more open-ended questions.)

12. Do not allow students access to back packs or their coats during an exam.

13. Be aware of technologies that could allow cheating, e.g. calculators, cell phones, pagers, etc.

14. Be explicit about possible sanctions. Have students refer to the Academic Honesty and Integrity Policy in their agenda books.

(Tom Solyom, personal communication, July 2006)

When academic dishonesty is suspected students can be interviewed privately in an attempt to determine whether the transgression was inadvertent or deliberate. If it was inadvertent the student may be counseled and may revise the work as appropriate; school/district policies generally dictate the response to deliberate dishonesty.

Effective policies first and foremost recognize that academic dishonesty is very serious inappropriate behavior equivalent to theft, and as such requires primarily behavioral consequences. These policies also recognize that academic dishonesty deprives everyone of quality evidence of student achievement. The appropriate assessment consequence is to have students redo the work with honesty and integrity.

The Archbishop Macdonald High School policy has the following possible sanctions:

> The grade coordinator in conjunction with the teacher, in whose class the offence occurred, has the authority to impose one or more of the following sanctions.

Plagiarism and/or Cheating

1. A student's academic misconduct will be confidentially communicated to all of his/her teachers.
2. At the teacher's discretion the students may be required to do another assignment/exam submitting their own original work for grading purposes.
3. The student must complete the exam/assignment on his or her own time (outside regular class time).
4. A zero may be awarded for that particular assignment/exam. In this instance, parents must be informed that the zero is being assigned as a punishment for inappropriate academic conduct and does not represent a true assessment of the student's ability. Assessment is a snapshot of performance, not potential. [This is not a procedure I recommend.]
5. All extracurricular involvement will be suspended until this sanction is lifted at the discretion of the disciplinary committee.
6. Probation—The probation period will last the remainder of the school year. If a student is discovered cheating and/or plagiarizing a second time during this period further sanctions will be applied.

In addition to the above sanctions, the grade coordinator, in conjunction with the school principal, has the authority to impose one or more of the following sanctions.

7. Suspension
8. Expulsion

(Archbishop Macdonald High School, 2006, pp. 26–27)

This sanction list is presented as an example, not as a model; note that the main behavioral consequence is suspension from all extracurricular involvement. This would be a significant consequence for participating students but not for nonparticipants. The policy could be reworded in the following way to avoid this potential problem:

1. (Entry 2)—Require students to redo the assignment/exam with the stated reason being "the provision of accurate evidence of achievement," not "grading purposes." This should not be at each teacher's discretion and probably should be done with supervision in or out of class time.

2. (Entry 4)—Do not include the option of zero. I would also prefer the use of the words "understanding, skill and/or knowledge" to replace "ability" and the last sentence should read, "A single assessment is a snapshot of performance, not a judgment of achievement."

3. (Entry 5)—For offences in the last month or two of the school year, probation probably should be extended for returning students for a period of time into the next school year.

Another important aspect of any school policy that involves judgment is that there must be an appeal process. There is such a process in the Archbishop Macdonald policy:

Appeal Process

Any student has the right to appeal the charges and/or sanctions determined by the teacher and grade coordinator within 1 week. The student will meet with the Appeal Board Committee, which will consist of the Principal, the subject Department Head, a counselor and, if requested, the student's parents. The student must fill out the appropriate form. The parents will be informed. (Archbishop Macdonald High School, 2006, p. 27)

Student Involvement

One way to involve students in academic honesty is for schools to have clear policies and to have frequent age-appropriate discussions about what this means, using specific examples. I have heard of some schools that have an honor code that requires students to attach a statement to all assessments that they have not cheated or plagiarized. Obviously this would not prevent academic dishonesty, but students who have to reflect on this issue for each assessment are likely to develop a clearer understanding of what academic honesty requires.

Summary

Academic dishonesty is unacceptable and must not be tolerated. But grades are broken if the response to cheating is a lowered score or grade, because this renders inaccurate the student's record of achievement. The fix is to remove grading as the vehicle for assigning a consequence to students who cheat, and to have an academic honesty policy that clearly describes inappropriate practices and the consequences for breaches. To emphasize that the learning is most important, the policy would also require that students must redo any assessment that involved academic dishonesty—without cheating or plagiarizing.

> *Don't use grades punitively. . . . Without exception, experts in the area of student grading recommend that grades not be used in a punitive sense. When a teacher uses grades as punishment for student behaviors, the teacher establishes an adversarial relationship in which grades are no longer meaningful to students as indicators of their accomplishment. The punitive use of grades only increases the likelihood that students will lose respect for the evaluation system; consequently the appeal to students of subverting such a system will be heightened. (Cizek, 2003, p. 100)*

Teacher Vignette

Bernie Soto, Science Department Head, Eastglen High School, Edmonton, Alberta, Grade 10 Science Class

Working our way through our chemistry unit, I announced the date for our chemistry unit final . . . a culminating summative assessment. I informed students that if they received their highest score on the culminating assessment, this would most likely become their unit mark. The students had worked their way through three shorter chapter assessments and of course many formative tasks and classroom observations so I had gathered quite a lot of information on how each student in the class was progressing. I was confident that if students were successful on this unit final, they would have indeed demonstrated the essential learning outcomes of the chemistry unit.

I informed some students individually of the need to come and see me for assistance with specific concepts prior to the final as they had struggled on previous assessments. While some students took advantage of the assistance the two students in this story did not. Both students had struggled on previous assessments with marks below 50 percent yet on the final assessment both scored marks in the high seventies. This result did not make sense based on my gradebook marks and observations.

I decided to have a conversation with both students individually. I began the conversation by informing the students of their results and how happy I was that they had demonstrated such a big improvement. However, I also let them know that I needed to be certain whether their achievement level was really what they demonstrated on the final. I required them to answer some basic chemistry questions that any student with a passing score should be able to answer. After 6–7 questions I found it quite easy to ascertain that indeed both students did not understand some basic chemistry concepts. After further questioning both confessed to having looked at an adjacent student's multiple-choice answer sheet for their responses. I informed both students that their Unit Final exam marks were invalid and that they would have to write an alternate assessment.

I informed their parents about the incident and suggested both students come in for remediation prior to writing the alternate assessment.

Further, I explained to both students that the difficulty would now lay in reestablishing trust. I informed them that the joy of teaching comes from having successful students and that from now on, rather than be happy for them when they did well on an assessment, I would have nagging doubts. Both agreed, as a condition of reestablishing that trust that they would sit at the front of their respective rows when writing future summative assessments.

In the end, both students came in for extra help, with both writing and passing the alternate assessment, although with marks in the fifties rather than high seventies. I was able to maintain a good working relationship with both students and both completed the course.

Policy Example

Limestone District School Board, ON—from the Assessment, Evaluation, and Reporting Insert in Student Planner

Academic Honesty Policy

Academic honesty is a core value in our school. If you submit work or parts of work that are not your own, you have not shown that you can demonstrate the curriculum expectations. Plagiarism is the theft of intellectual property and is treated with the utmost seriousness. To avoid this, your teachers will help you plan your work. If you find that you require assistance in order to complete the assignment properly, see your teacher well in advance of the due date. Your teacher can help you to establish a reasonable timeline to complete an assignment and/or strategies to do your research and write your final submission. Remember when you do research, that you must cite all sources. See the information at the end of this section for citation rules and methods.

Plagiarism

In a case where a teacher suspects plagiarism, the teacher will determine the scope of plagiarism that has taken place. For intentional and/or excessive cases where you have submitted work that is clearly not your own, the teacher will speak to you and will refer the matter to administration. A meeting will then be organized by school administration. All or some of the following parties will be asked to attend: you, your parent or guardian, the teacher, a department head, a student services representative, and an administrator. For cases where it is deemed that plagiarism has taken place, the following steps will apply:

- For a first offense, an in-school suspension of one day will be assigned, during which you may have to complete, under supervision, an assignment based on the overall expectations addressed in the original assignment. You may have to complete an additional paper on the subject of academic ethics and honesty. A record of the plagiarism will be kept centrally in the main office until you leave the school permanently.

- A second or subsequent offense may result in a longer out-of-school suspension and/or removal from the course.

Unauthorized Sharing of Work

Providing work to another student for the purposes of academic dishonesty is a violation of our code of conduct.

If you allow another student to use your work and present it as his or her own, you will be referred to administration and serve an academic detention where a paper on academic ethics may be assigned.

If you use another student's work and present it as your own, you will be required to:

- demonstrate the expectations covered by the test or assignment in another way, to be determined by the teacher.

- serve an in-school suspension where a paper on academic ethics may be written.

A record will be kept centrally in the main office and consequences will be more severe for subsequent infractions, which may include a longer suspension and/or removal from the course.

Don't consider attendance in grade determination; report absences separately.

Excused and unexcused absences are not relevant to an achievement grade. There is no legitimate purpose for distinguishing between excused and unexcused absences. For educational purposes, therefore, there need only to be recorded absences.

—*Gathercoal, 2004, p. 163*

*G*rades are broken when they are directly or indirectly related to a student's attendance record. The simple fix requires absences be reported separately from grades, and that grades be determined only from evidence of achievement.

Most teachers would probably agree that all students should attend school regularly. Most students need to do so to be successful in their learning. However, standards-based learning is not about seat time. It is about what students know, understand, and can do. Grades should be accurate reflections of that and that alone. Attendance therefore is best recorded and reported separately simply as days present (or days absent).

It is common for schools/districts to go to great lengths to distinguish between excused and unexcused absences, with the difference having a significant impact on grades and the ability of students to "make up" for absences. The distinction between excused and unexcused absences may be very important for behavioral and legal reasons, but it is irrelevant to learning and assessment perspectives. From these perspectives, the only issue is whether students learn and demonstrate it by providing appropriate assessment evidence. Students who have been absent require opportunities to learn what they have missed and subsequently to demonstrate what they know, understand, and can do, regardless of the reason for the absence.

Another reason it is inappropriate to make this distinction is that the difference often depends on the "creativity" of the parent(s) or the student. This is a polite way of saying whether parents or students are willing to lie, which is obviously an inappropriate basis for decisions affecting grades or "makeup" opportunities.

In some of the schools in which I taught it was a common practice (especially in physical education) to include a fixed number of points for attendance and to deduct one or two points for each absence. In subjects such as physical education, drama, and music active participation is essential, but with such a procedure a student would have zero for attendance after 10 absences even though they attended 35 out of 45 days in the grading period. Such procedures are illogical, distort the meaning of the grade, and should not be permitted.

One aspect of attendance and grades that presents a real dilemma is when there are requirements that students attend certain out-of-school activities or performances, such as concerts in a music course or performances in a drama course. When participation is required, however, for the program to function, it is reasonable to suggest that there should be consequences for failure to attend. Policies that simply state that students receive a failing grade if they miss performances are inappropriate. A student who is proficient or better in all the music or drama learning goals would have their grade distorted if it was lowered for failing to attend one or more performances. The best approach in standards-based schools is probably a behavioral consequence but I acknowledge that it is difficult to determine what is appropriate. As schools/districts make the transition to a true standards base it may be necessary to establish a policy that students must attend X (or all) concerts/performances as a prerequisite to receiving a grade/credit, and that they will otherwise receive an Incomplete. This policy can be communicated in writing to students and parents at or before the start of the course.

Summary

In standards-based systems all marks and grades (pass/fail, A/B/C/D/F, etc.) should be determined by proficiency, not by seat time. Most students need to attend class to be successful and teachers must ensure that engaging learning activities are being provided so that students feel it is worth their while to attend. However, absences should not directly affect students' grades. Grades are broken if there is a direct impact because a behavioral variable is being allowed to distort achievement. The fix is to deal with attendance separately from achievement by simply reporting days present (or days absent).

> *I was confronted at a workshop by a teacher who asked "are you telling me that if a student has been ill and another has been skipping, that they both should be able to make up the work missed?" My response was that both needed an educator when they returned, perhaps the one who skipped more than the other. Regardless of the reason for student absences, make up work and late assignments should be accepted to ensure those students equal educational opportunity. (Gathercoal, 2004, p. 163)*

Teacher Vignettes

Jon Wickert, Caesar Rodney High School

I have a student whose mother became very ill at the beginning of our third marking period. As this is a low-income family, it had a dramatic effect on her responsibilities at home and on her emotional stability. This student essentially shut down and stopped turning in work and attending school. I tried hard for about 4 weeks to find out what was going on. The school would not tell me for confidentiality reasons but I finally got this young lady to tell me about her situation. Once I knew, I told her that we could be flexible when it came to getting her work turned in as long as she showed that she was progressing in the completion of her assignments. I gave her the extension on assignments all the way back to the beginning of the marking period. Eventually her mother returned home but was still very ill and it fell on this student to get her sisters and nieces to day care at 8 AM, which meant she was late to my class every single day for over 12 weeks. She finally got caught up and turned in all assignments for both marking periods. She finished with a 92 percent for the marking period.

When students want to achieve and we provide them the opportunity, even in the face of sometimes insurmountable odds, we at least give them a chance when we do not use absences against them. If I were to count all of these absences against her, she would have had to repeat the course and possibly would have dropped out because the school policy is if it is an excused absence, they receive 1 day per day of absence to make the work up; if it is unexcused, they do not have to be given the opportunity to make it up and if they miss 10 days per semester course or 20 per full year course they are denied credit.

Sheri Tchir, Eastglen High School, Edmonton, Alberta

In my experience, teachers are well intentioned when they include attendance in a student's grade. There is this misconception that this will bring more students to class more often. I have found the reverse to be true. Students miss class for a variety of reasons—most of which we have no influence over. There is a whole world they are involved in that we only get a partial glimpse of when they are sitting in our classroom. Using grades to shape behaviour, lates, and attendance simply has not worked in my experience. We might think it is working because our high achievers attend regularly, but we really cannot say one is the cause of the other. My most serious attendance concerns are about students who, for whatever reason, feel like there is no point coming to class if they are already failing. In my experience, grading attendance is not what brings students to class. I can think of more than a few students who started coming more regularly when I sought them out and explained that there was still hope for success. They could catch up and still pass. This is where I have seen the most difference.

We need to look for other methods to motivate students to come to class. Most students soon face the natural consequence if they are not in class for the formative work, as they have great difficulty being successful on the summative assessments. Granted, it sometimes takes time and overcoming obstacles. For example, I have a student who repeatedly tells me he does not need to write down notes or complete the learning activities. This same student has some difficulty with attendance. He says, "It's all in here"—pointing to his head. I also get comments like, "Don't worry, I know this." So we decided we would wait until his first major summative assessment and see how that was working. The truth is even if I have doubts, there is the possibility he does have the expected knowledge and skills. Maybe he does not need to practice or even attend to be successful. This might bruise my ego as a teacher but it is entirely possible. So we waited; he did not pass. Before I could even initiate a conversation, he came to me and said, "I know. This isn't working." That's all it took. Attendance and work improved because he now saw the purpose of it. I admit that watching your students make mistakes is difficult, but having the patience to wait it out, combined with using other strategies that do not involve grading, usually pays off. Even though attendance and formative work were not factored into his grade, I did address them in other ways, such as phone calls home, e-mails, and sometimes involving the school administration. Just because something is not scored, does not mean it is not important. I find this seems to be a prominent concern for teachers. This same student started completing formative work and has just written another summative assessment. This time he was successful.

Policy Example

Bremerton School District, WA

4. Attendance

Attendance is a behavior issue and should not be used in determining student grades. Performance-based course participation requirements, approved by the Bremerton School District Instructional Council, will be clearly stated for earning of course credit/pass at Bremerton High School and Mountain View Middle School. As an example for music participation (the prerequisite) requirement might be: student must attend 3 of the 4 concerts during the semester to earn a choir credit.

Don't include group scores in grades; use only individual achievement evidence.

Group scores [grades] are so blatantly unfair that on this basis alone they should never be used.

—Kagan, 1995, p. 69

*G*rades are broken when they include group scores from work done in cooperative learning groups. The fix is to ensure that all evidence used to determine grades comes from individual evidence of achievement.

Cooperative learning is a very powerful teaching/learning strategy; done well and used appropriately it can lead to significant learning gains and improve attitudes about learning and school. But frequently in cooperative learning situations students are required to produce a group product or presentation for which they receive a group score, which is then recorded for each member of the group. This is an inappropriate practice, as illustrated in the "For Better or For Worse" cartoon in Figure 2.4.

In Figure 2.5, Spencer Kagan provides seven specific reasons for opposing group scores (grades). His first four reasons are clearly illustrated in Figure 2.4. The situation depicted is obviously unfair, as one student is receiving "credit" for something she didn't do; report cards will be "debased" because these students will receive inaccurate grades; this situation would undermine motivation because the next time these students will feel that their effort is of

Figure 2.4   An Example of an Inappropriate Group Scoring Practice

Figure 2.5   Kagan's Seven Reasons for Opposing Group Scores (Grades)

Group scores (grades)

1. Are no(t) fair
2. Debase report cards
3. Undermine motivation
4. Convey the wrong message
5. Violate individual accountability
6. Are responsible for resistance to cooperative learning
7. May be challenged in court

Source: The information in Figure 2.5 is adapted from "Group Grades Miss the Mark," by S. Kagan, 1995, *Educational Leadership, 52(8),* pp. 69–70. Adapted by permission of Association for Supervision and Curriculum Development.

dubious value; and this group score sends the wrong message about the purpose and value of teamwork.

But the two most important reasons why group scores should not be used as part of student grades are reasons 5 and 6. With regard to reason 5, many models of cooperative learning (see, e.g., Gibbs, 2000; Johnson & Johnson, 2004; Kagan, 1995) have individual accountability as a basic principle in the model. Group scores that become part of individual grade determination violate this principle, meaning the cooperative learning model is being implemented incorrectly. Regarding reason 6, not surprisingly, cooperative learning has encountered parental and student resistance in some schools/ districts precisely because of group scoring. In the extreme, parents have taken teachers, principals, schools, and districts to court over this issue. The parents generally have won because judges followed the principle that no student's grade should depend on the achievement (or behavior) of other students. Cooperative learning can be a powerful teaching/learning strategy. We want to help students to be successful learners so we need to have all such powerful strategies available. We do not want to impair any strategy's effectiveness by incorrectly measuring the achievement of students who use it.

There is yet another issue with giving scores for products or performance developed in cooperative learning groups. The strategy is cooperative *learning*, which implies that any activities that occur in groups are learning activities and any assessment of them is best considered formative assessment—to help students improve their knowledge, understanding, and skill(s). Such assessment is for learning and should not produce scores that are part of grade determination. (This issue is the subject of Fix 13.)

Summary

Grades are broken if they involve the use of group scores from cooperative learning or group activities. This is so because the group scores may not accurately reflect the achievement of each student and therefore would be unfair for some members of the group. This problem can be addressed by recognizing that cooperative learning is essentially a learning activity, *not* an assessment tool. After a class has experienced cooperative learning teachers can then assess students individually to find out what they know, understand, and can do as a result. This individual assessment could involve one or more of the following: "teacher monitoring of [cooperative] activity work; an essay response based on questions formulated during the activity; a class discussion of the questions and responses generated; [or a test] on the content of the questions formulated and responses generated" (Benevino & Snodgrass, 1998, p. 146).

> *The assessment of individuals within groups begins with setting individual learning goals and involves such procedures as individual tests and products, observing students while working in groups, giving group members a questionnaire to complete, and interviewing group members during group sessions. There is a pattern to classroom life summarized as "learn it in a group, perform it alone." (Johnson & Johnson, 2004, p. 53, emphasis added)*

Teacher Vignette

Sheri Tchir, Eastglen High School, Edmonton, Alberta

Group work and cooperation is essential to learning. The benefits are indisputable; however, the problems associated with it are not new. If our primary objective is to assess the individual student on curricular objectives, how can we incorporate group processes? I have struggled with this dilemma and through trial and error and with student input I have come to something that seems to work. In my classroom, students do several group projects, activities, and debates, but it is all "learning" and assessment is formative. To measure each individual's actual knowledge or skill, every project has an individual, summative component. This could be a piece of writing, a discussion, or a series of questions during a presentation. I need to know what each student has learned. I cannot assume from a PowerPoint® presentation or poster, that each individual contributed a certain amount. I cannot even assume those students did all the work on their own. The only judgment I can make to determine a grade comes from what the student communicates to me on his or her own. I have had colleagues question if anyone even completes the project if it is not for their grade, or ask why a student would put effort in producing a high-quality project. The students rarely ask these questions. In fact, they *ask* to do group projects and they do complete them to a relatively high standard. For them this is a powerful and enjoyable way to learn. I repeatedly find on exams that students almost always do very well on the questions that related to their project topic. I share this information with my students, even before the project as it is a pattern that repeats itself. This seems to be motivation for most.

Policy Example

St. Michaels University School, Victoria, BC

8. Group work

Cooperative learning is a valuable instructional tool for developing life skills, but it is not an assessment tool. Students will be given ample opportunity to work experientially and collaboratively, but will be *graded individually*. Learning from others and helping others learn are both essential elements of the learning community at SMUS. As SMUS students reside across a wide geographical area and come from a diverse socioeconomic background, group activities should be confined to class time and require a limited amount of resources (or the required resources should be provided).

Chapter 3

Fixes for Low-Quality or Poorly Organized Evidence

Fixes

7   Don't organize information in grading records by assessment methods or simply summarize into a single grade; organize and report evidence by standards/learning goals.

8   Don't assign grades using inappropriate or unclear performance standards; provide clear descriptions of achievement expectations.

9   Don't assign grades based on a student's achievement compared to other students; compare each student's performance to preset standards.

10   Don't rely on evidence gathered using assessments that fail to meet standards of quality; rely only on quality assessments.

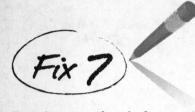

Fix 7

Don't organize information in grading records by assessment methods or simply summarize into a single grade; organize and report evidence by standards/learning goals.

The important thing is . . . that everyone in the [school or] district . . . can identify what it is that students are expected to learn.

—*Butler & McMunn, 2006, p. 23*

*G*rades are broken when evidence of learning from multiple sources is blended into a single grade and the communication fails to show how successful students have been in mastering individual standards/learning goals. The fix is to base grades on published school/district/state standards (learning outcomes/goals, essential learnings, expectations, strands, etc.), and to report them for each standard to create a more complete profile of individual student strengths and weaknesses. Evidence also may be summarized into a grade, and often this is required. But the total communication must also and always report mastery by standard or by some categories derived from the standards.

This requires curriculum, instruction, assessment, *and* grading and reporting all to be organized around the standards. Many schools have successfully done so with curriculum and instruction and increasingly assessment has become aligned as well. However, while many schools/districts have embraced standards-based grading and reporting at the elementary level, there remains much work to be done, especially in middle and high schools. Schools focused on standards only for curriculum, instruction, and assessment are standards *referenced*, not standards *based*.

Traditionally, teachers have organized their evidence of student achievement for all learning goals either simply in the order collected over time or in categories based on the type of data, such as tests, projects, and homework assignments. For each collection, they then distill the individual scores into a single summary grade and report that grade. In either case, what is not recorded and therefore not reported is vital information revealing how well each student has mastered each learning goal. In other words, although each student's performance can be summarized with a single symbol/grade, this approach provides no basis for reporting direct evidence of student performance on each learning goal, unless accompanied by a narrative report that describes learning in relation to the written curriculum. To be standards based in grading, teachers plan each assessment to provide direct evidence of student proficiency on specific learning outcomes/goals and then record this evidence by goal, dedicating columns or blocks of space in their gradebook to each learning goal. Figure 3.1 shows a sample of such a gradebook using some of the State of Oregon reading standards for Grade 4. The standards are the basis for organizing assessments and collecting evidence from tests and performance assessments ("PA" in the figure) to determine an overall grade (if necessary) and a grade for each standard.

In this example the first test was not just 10 questions worth 2 points each with a single score recorded and reported as X out of 20; the test elicited information on two of the five standards shown, and our example student received scores of 15 out of 20 on understanding text read and 19 out of 20 on identifying key facts and information. Because the main use of these scores is to determine proficiency they are recorded respectively as a 3 (for proficient) and 4 (for excelling). (See Fix 8 for more on performance standards.) The performance assessment (PA) provided level scores for three

Figure 3.1   Sample Summary of Evidence for Meeting State of Oregon Reading Standards

Student:

Achievement Evidence											
Assessments → Standards ↓	9/1 Test	9/8 PA									**Summary**
Read aloud grade level text											
Understand, learn and use new vocabulary											
Listen to, read and understand text	15/20	4									
Identify key facts and information	19/20	3									
Identify and analyze text that uses sequential order		4									
Comments:	*The standards used here have been selected and adapted from the Oregon Grade 4 reading strand.*										

Report Card Grade	
Most consistent level of achievement	

Note: The Oregon reading standards appear at www.ode.state.or.us/teachlearn/real/standards/searchablestandards.aspx.

standards using a 5-level rubric (0–4). This gradebook format enables teachers and students (and parents) to see a profile of student performance that clearly identifies areas of strength and areas for improvement.

Often at the middle and high school levels, where teachers interact with a large number of students, teachers feel/believe that recording data at the learning goal level is impractical. An alternative approach is to use strands within a subject as the organizing structure. Guskey and Bailey (2010, p. 43) make the distinction between "curriculum standards" (that are many and detailed and frequently expressed in "educator language") and "reporting stan-

Figure 3.2 Sample Summary of Evidence for Meeting State of Florida Grade 6 Mathematics Standards, First Grading Period

Student:

	Achievement Evidence												
Assessments → Standards ↓	8/13 Test	8/20 PA	8/23 PA	8/24 PA	8/25 Test	8/30 PA	9/5 Test	9/8 PA	9/12 Test	9/19 PA	9/21 PA	9/23 Exam	SUMMARY
Number Sense, Concepts and Operations			2		11/20 (1)		16/20 (3)			2		7/10 (2)	C
Measurement	19/20 (4)	4			18/20 (4)			4			4	16/20 (3)	A
Geometry and Spatial Sense		4		2		3	17/20 (3)				3	10/10 (4)	B
Functions, Patterns, and Relationships	11/20 (1)	2				2				2		14/20 (2)	C
Data Analysis, Probability, and Statistics		1		2		3	20/20 (4)			4		19/20 (4)	A

Overall Grade	A

Note: The Florida Mathematics standards can be found at www.floridastandards .org/Standards/FLStandardSearch.aspx

dards" (that are few and broader and should be expressed in parent-friendly language).

Figure 3.2 illustrates what such a standards-based gradebook might look like for an individual student over a grading period. The top row of numbers is the date of the assessment. Each test (T) and performance assessment (PA) is recorded by strand. Some provide evidence of only one strand; other, more comprehensive assessments provide evidence on several strands. By the end of the grading period there are at least five scores for each strand, which is sufficient evidence to make summary judgments for that strand. All performance scores/marks must be recorded using a common scale, so tests scored using points are recorded using the same five-point scale used for the performance assessments. If a single summary grade for the subject is required this can be determined by identifying the most consistent level or calculating central tendency (mean, median, or mode). When students perform at the same level on all strands, the summary grade is easy to determine and has clear meaning. But if a student's mastery is inconsistent, then a summary grade is difficult to determine and will lack the detail needed to understand the student's real achievement; that is, their strengths and weaknesses. It is for this reason that I recommend that we always report information about the level of achievement on each standard, backed up by summary subject grades (if required).

These gradebook examples show one page for each student because this is the best way to illustrate this Fix and it is also the best way to collect evidence of student achievement. However, teachers interacting with a large number of students or teaching several subjects to a smaller number of students may find one page per student to be impractical, and may prefer gradebooks such as the one shown in Figure 3.3.

Figure 3.3 shows part of the gradebook that Glenda Greier used in her Grade 3 and 4 classes in Bay District Schools in Panama City, Florida. There is a column for two of the math strands on this page. Two additional pages are used for the other math strands, with space for each student in her class on each page. Note also that Ms. Greier recorded separately information from formative and summative assessments (Fix 13 covers this issue in detail).

Another approach that may work well for some teachers and subjects is a blending of the two approaches described here. For example, there are five strands in the U.S. foreign language standards: (1) Communication, (2) Cultures, (3) Connections, (4) Comparisons, and (5) Communities (Standards for Foreign Language Learning, n.d.). Communication has three standards: 1 requires students to engage in conversations; 2 requires students to understand and interpret written and spoken language; and 3 requires students to present information,

Figure 3.3 Mrs. Greier's Gradebook

Mrs. Greier's Gradebook
2005–2006

Math	Number Sense, Concepts, & Operation				Measurement			
	Formative		Summative		Formative		Summative	
Date								
SSS/GLE								
Methods								
Students								
1.								
2.								
3.								
4.								
5.								
6.								
7.								
8.								
9.								
10.								
11.								
12.								
13.								
14.								
15.								
16.								
17.								
18.								
19.								
20.								
21.								
22.								
23.								
24.								
25.								
26.								
27.								
28.								
29.								
30.								

Source: Copyright © 2005 by Glenda Greier. Reprinted by permission.

concepts, and ideas to an audience of listeners or readers. There is a distinct likelihood that some students would achieve very differently on each of these. So for effective communication and instructional decision making, a foreign language teacher records information about achievement on each of these standards separately, but it may be sufficient for the other strands to collect and report information at the strand level. The level of specificity at which teachers collect evidence depends on the nature of the learning goals, the specificity of reporting required, and the teacher's beliefs about what is both necessary and possible. (Examples of gradebooks at different levels of specificity appear in Stiggins et al., 2004, pp. 289 & 290.)

Many, maybe even most, teachers now use computer grading software to (help) manage evidence of student achievement; almost all computer grading programs can be used for standards-based grading because these programs rely on "bins," or categories. Teachers have generally made those bins tests, projects, homework assignments, and so on, but they may just as easily be standards or strands. The only limitation is the number of bins or categories allowed by the program. The computer grading program that I endorse because it supports teachers in their use of standards-based practices is PowerTeacher, developed by the PowerSchool division of Pearson. So, wherever teachers are on the technological continuum, from hardcopy paper gradebook to computer software to using one's own spreadsheet, they can put this Fix in place. There may be a lot of work involved at first to get organized to record scores and deter-mine grades in this way. However, teachers then find that assessment and grading are easier to organize, as they are "working smarter, not harder," using the same organizing structure right through the process and not using one structure for curriculum, instruction, and assessment and a different structure for grading and reporting.

Summary

Grades are broken when they are not directly based on standards and do not give information about achievement of standards. Fixing this requires the use of standards-based curriculum, instruction, and assessment, and collecting and reporting student achievement by standards. Teachers should collect information about student achievement of individual learning goals and should be able to discuss this information with students and parents. For report card purposes, learning goals may be grouped together to summarize student achievement.

> *The principal limitation of any grading system that requires the teacher to assign one number or letter to represent course learning is that one symbol can convey only one meaning. . . . One symbol cannot do justice to the different degrees of learning a student acquires across all learning outcomes. (Tombari & Borich, 1999, p. 213)*

Teacher Vignettes

Peter Round, High School Vice Principal, Jakarta International School

Reorganizing how I record assessment evidence in my gradebook along the lines suggested by Fix 7 has transformed the feedback I can offer to students and parents. Instead of "Quiz 1, Test 2, Lab 4 etc" headings, I now classify all learning goals into six categories (Knowledge, Application, Scientific Reasoning, Design, Data Collection and Processing, and Conclusion and Evaluation) and break down each assessment into these categories. Feedback following an assessment is consequently more focused, specific, and more useful to plan next steps in learning for the student, parent, and myself.

Mike Musil, English teacher, North Star High School, Lincoln Public Schools, NE

Once I started using standards-based grading, parent-teacher conferences became completely different. No longer was I talking about things like missing homework. Now we were talking about what the student knew. Parents left with a sense of hope rather than a sense of despair.

Assessments are now broken down into standards and objectives, and it's tightened up instruction; I'm forced to ask myself, why am I teaching this? If I teach Julius Caesar, I'd better be doing it for more than just discussion purposes in an English classroom.

Policy Example

Bay District Schools, Panama City, Florida

Principle 4. Grading is fair, consistent, and meaningful.

Guideline 4.1: Teachers determine grades based on individual achievement of content standards.

- The teacher carefully designs assessments to closely align with the learning target.
- The teacher determines achievement of standards for each individual student. Group scores are not used for individual grading.

Guideline 4.2: Teachers inform students about grading criteria and methods used for determining grades.

- At the beginning of the lesson or unit, the teacher explains the grading criteria with the students.
    - The criteria are specific and related to the targeted benchmark(s).
    - If possible, the students are given copies of the criteria.
- The teacher should explain the assessment method that will be used to determine the student's grade (i.e., essay questions, open response, open-book, performance, etc.)

Guideline 4.3: Teachers use predetermined and consistent grading procedures in the same courses and across grade levels.

- Teachers of the same course and/or grade level meet and compare assessments and student results on a regular basis.
    - They have a common understanding of what mastery of their course standards looks like based on district expectations.
    - They share exemplars, anchors, assessments, and scoring tools as appropriate to increase their understanding of what quality student work should reflect.

Fix 8

Don't assign grades using inappropriate or unclear performance standards; provide clear descriptions of achievement expectations.

Performance standards specify "how good is good enough." They relate to issues of assessment that gauge the degree to which content standards have been attained. . . . They are indices of quality that specify how adept or competent a student demonstration should be.

—Kendall & Marzano, 1997, pp. 16–17

*G*rades are broken when they are determined using poorly defined performance standards, such as letter–number relationships (A = 90–100, B = 80–89, etc.), that have traditionally masqueraded as performance standards. The fix is to develop clear and rich criterion-referenced descriptions of a limited number of levels of achievement. Whatever symbols are used to summarize student achievement (e.g., A B C D F; 4 3 2 1; E M N U), each level must be described clearly, with the level considered "good enough" (i.e., competent, proficient, mastered) precisely identified.

The judgments made when developing the descriptors and when evaluating student work are always subjective. These are not matters of learning science, but are common communication conventions. As long as everyone involved accepts that those who have developed the descriptors and levels are qualified, and understands the terms used, we can communicate effectively.

The best performance-standard setting (determining how good is good enough) pools the collective experience of a number of educators who are knowledgeable and experienced. When teams of teachers address performance standards together, they can develop the basis for communicating achievement continua for each standard in ways that all concerned will understand, including students and their families. In that context, the teams also can set performance standards at the appropriate level along each continuum. Once developed, the resulting depiction of academic success will be published and public for all—administrators, teachers, students, parents, and others—to see from the beginning of instruction. Given that states and provinces tend to specify content standards, this work is best done at the state/provincial level, but if it has not been, it should be done at the district level.

Once the performance standards are in place, teachers need frequent opportunities for professional dialogue about them so they develop shared understanding and apply them consistently. Darling-Hammond (2010) notes in a paper for the Council of Chief State School Officers that effective assessment systems "engage teachers in scoring student work based on shared targets" (p. 5). She states further, "Most successful systems in the U.S. and other high-achieving nations invest in extensive moderation to ensure an accurate, reliable, and consistent scoring process and enable teachers to deeply understand the standards and develop stronger curriculum and instruction. The moderated scoring process is a strong professional learning experience, and as teachers become more skilled at using new assessment practices and developing curriculum, they become more effective at teaching the standards" (p. 8). This points to the need for districts and schools to put a lot of time (and money) into such opportunities at the school and district level.

In a pure standards-based system we would only have two levels of performance—proficient and not proficient. Some schools/districts use only these two levels, but this is rare. Most commonly, performance continua use at least four levels: (1) a level above proficient, to recognize (and encourage) excellence; (2) proficient; (3) below proficient but acceptable; and (4) significantly below proficiency, or insufficient. Once we agree on the number of levels we determine the characteristics of each level and label and describe them clearly and concisely. As much as possible the language chosen should be descriptive, not judgmental. Figure 3.4 shows one example (see Arter & Chappuis, 2006, for a variety of other examples).

It is important to note that the terms used in Figure 3.4 describe the quality of achievement on the learning goals in the public, published curriculum in terms of the knowledge and skills demonstrated at the time of the report card. There are two important aspects to this—the meaning of quality and the timing. With regard to the former, as noted previously, Guskey (2004) illustrates very clearly that we have alternatives. With regard to the latter, Figure 3.4, for example, states directly that the levels describe performance at the time of the report card. The alternative is to consider the standard to be the performance level expected at the end of the year. This choice must be made and communicated clearly to teachers, students, and parents. If the choice is year-end performance levels, everyone involved, especially parents, must be helped to understand that there will be few, if any, proficient grades on report cards until near the end of the year.

The challenge is to create clear descriptors of our overall levels so that we have a delineated achievement continuum within which we can consistently judge student achievement to be competent or to deserve a certain grade. It must, however, be emphasized that the overall performance standard is only a starting point in the standards-setting process. The most important performance standards are those used to give students feedback and/or scores on their demonstrations of learning. Thus when the overall performance levels and descriptors have been accepted, standard-specific classroom rubrics and performance standards must be developed using the language of the standard. Then these rubrics, written in the actual language that describes levels of achievement for the subject and

Figure 3.4   Edmonton (AB) Catholic Elementary Schools Levels
of Achievement (Performance Standards)

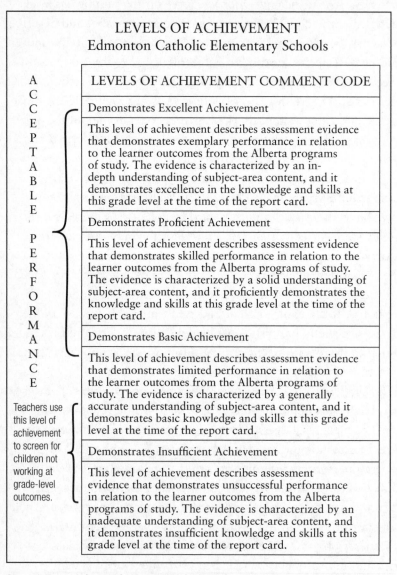

LEVELS OF ACHIEVEMENT
Edmonton Catholic Elementary Schools

A C C E P T A B L E P E R F O R M A N C E	LEVELS OF ACHIEVEMENT COMMENT CODE
	Demonstrates Excellent Achievement
	This level of achievement describes assessment evidence that demonstrates exemplary performance in relation to the learner outcomes from the Alberta programs of study. The evidence is characterized by an in-depth understanding of subject-area content, and it demonstrates excellence in the knowledge and skills at this grade level at the time of the report card.
	Demonstrates Proficient Achievement
	This level of achievement describes assessment evidence that demonstrates skilled performance in relation to the learner outcomes from the Alberta programs of study. The evidence is characterized by a solid understanding of subject-area content, and it proficiently demonstrates the knowledge and skills at this grade level at the time of the report card.
	Demonstrates Basic Achievement
	This level of achievement describes assessment evidence that demonstrates limited performance in relation to the learner outcomes from the Alberta programs of study. The evidence is characterized by a generally accurate understanding of subject-area content, and it demonstrates basic knowledge and skills at this grade level at the time of the report card.
	Demonstrates Insufficient Achievement
	This level of achievement describes assessment evidence that demonstrates unsuccessful performance in relation to the learner outcomes from the Alberta programs of study. The evidence is characterized by an inadequate understanding of subject-area content, and it demonstrates insufficient knowledge and skills at this grade level at the time of the report card.

Teachers use this level of achievement to screen for children not working at grade-level outcomes.

Source: Copyright © Edmonton Catholic School District, Edmonton, Alberta, Canada. Reprinted by permission.

grade-level standard, need to be supported by exemplars demonstrating levels at, above, and below proficiency. Again the best classroom performance–standard setting process pools the collective experience of several educators. These teachers, confident, competent masters of the relevant academic discipline who have extensive teaching experience, set standards based on their collective study of samples of student work. Here again, teachers using these standards need frequent opportunities for professional dialogue about them so they develop shared understanding and apply them consistently. Figure 3.5 presents an example of a classroom performance standard.

The performance standards, rubrics, and exemplars need to be published and public for all to see from the beginning of instruction. The key to success is to describe levels of achievement in terms of the characteristics of the actual kind of academic achievement (or behaviors) being judged. Obviously, therefore, performance standards for feedback and scoring will be very different for different contexts (subjects and grade levels). When such descriptions are accompanied by samples of student work depicting each level of proficiency, we lay a solid foundation for effective judgment of and communication about student achievement.

As professional associations of teachers have established standards and associated performance continua for their particular academic disciplines, and as state assessments have been created that represent the state's standards, all involved have had to decide, How good is good enough? We should rely on these resources whenever available to assist with local standard setting.

After the performance standards are in place, understood, and used competently, in almost all schools summary grades have to be determined and communicated to students, parents, and other interested parties. This requires that teachers use quality assessment (Fix 10) and combine the evidence of each student's achievement in appropriate ways (see especially Fixes 11, 12, 13, and 14). Traditionally, especially at the middle and high school levels, this has involved grading scales that have linked letter grades with

Figure 3.5   Oral Presentation Rubric

Score	Language	Delivery	Organization
A = 5	Correct grammar and pronunciation are used. Word choice is interesting and appropriate. Unfamiliar terms are defined in the context of the speech.	The voice demonstrates control with few distractions. The presentation holds the listener's attention. The volume and rate are at acceptable levels. Eye contact with the audience is maintained.	The message is organized. The speaker sticks to the topic. The main points are developed. It is easy to summarize the content of the speech.
B = 4 C = 3	Correct grammar and pronunciation are used. Word choice is adequate and understandable. Unfamiliar terms are not explained in the context of the speech. There is a heavy reliance on the listener's prior knowledge.	The voice is generally under control. The speaker can be heard and understood. The speaker generally maintains eye contact with the audience.	The organization is understandable. Main points may be underdeveloped. The speaker may shift unexpectedly from one point to another, but the message remains comprehensible. The speech can be summarized.
D = 2 F = 1	Errors in grammar and pronunciation occur. Word choice lacks clarity. The speaker puts the responsibility for understanding on the listener.	The student's voice is poor. The volume may be too low and the rate too fast. There may be frequent pauses. Nonverbal behaviors tend to interfere with the message.	Ideas are listed without logical sequence. The relationships between ideas are not clear. The student strays from the stated topic. It is difficult to summarize the speech.

Source: Adapted from "Rubric Sampler" (CD-ROM p. 52), in *Classroom Assessment for Student Learning: Doing It Right—Using It Well* by R. J. Stiggins, J. A. Arter, J. Chappuis, and S. Chappuis, 2004, Portland, OR: Assessment Training Institute. Copyright © 2010, 2006, 2004 by Pearson. Adapted by permission of Pearson. Original source unknown.

percentages. This has, in effect, created both a system of 101 levels and the illusion that grades are mathematically precise. An effective standards-based system should be built on a limited number of clearly described levels based on proficiency or quality. This means that to be consistent with a standards-based system *the use of the percentage system should be eliminated.* However, partly because of our traditional use of the percentage system and partly because some aspects of learning are quantifiable, we do need at times to be able to show the relationships between qualitative performance standards and quantity (see Arter & Chappuis, 2006; Stiggins, 2005). Figure 3.6 shows an example of this relationship. Note that the figure offers a sort of thesaurus to clarify the meaning of each level; the numbers and symbols are there, but as reference points only.

When we deemphasize the percentage system both our performance standards and the way we report student achievement will be clearer, more consistent, and richer in specific detail. As an added benefit, their clarity and specificity may make them effective teaching—and learning—tools, partly because a credit will no longer be defined simply as obtaining a mean of 50 or 60 percent. As Cooper (2010, p. 188) points out, "Knowing 50 percent of the material taught can hardly be considered 'proficient.' Nobody wants to fly with a pilot who scored 50 percent on his or her exams in flight training school. Pass/fail cut points of 50 percent (or 60 percent) are an outdated relic of norm-referenced approaches to grading." In standards-based systems passing and moving on to the next level of

Figure 3.6 Edmonton (AB) Catholic Elementary Schools—
Aligning Achievement Indicators

Wow	*Yes*	*Yes, but*	*No, but*
Excellent	**Proficient**	**Minimal**	**Insufficient**
Exceptional Exemplary Advanced High quality Superb Outstanding In-depth	Adept Skilled Solid Appropriate Capable	Basic Limited Minimally acceptable	Partial Beginning Approaching Well below Below Misperceptions Omissions Errors
4	3	2	1
A	B	C	N

Source: Copyright © 2006 Edmonton Catholic School District, Edmonton, Alberta, Canada. Reprinted by permission.

study should require mastery of performance standards that define this precisely.

It is also important to recognize that performance standards are about *achievement*, not about growth or progress. For example, a student could make significant personal growth while making limited progress at a (relatively) low level of achievement; also a student could make little growth while making limited progress at a (relatively) high level of achievement. Achievement, growth, and progress are closely related but different concepts (Figure 3.7). Achievement is an absolute and is the grading variable (the basic ingredient of grades); growth

Figure 3.7   **Definitions and Examples of Achievement, Growth, and Progress**

Achievement

"The act of achieving or performing; an obtaining by exertion; successful performance."

Measured as an absolute, e.g., "he/she . . . is 4 feet 6 inches tall" . . . "is reading at grade 2 level"

"Achievement at . . ."

Growth

"The process of growing: increase in size, number, frequency, strength, etc."

Measured against where a child was, e.g., "he/she . . . grew three inches since last measurement" . . . "has moved from grade 1 level in the last month"

"Growth from . . ."

Progress

"Movement, as toward a goal; advance."

Relative achievement measured against a goal, standard, future result, e.g., "he/she . . . is now one inch below average height for age" . . . "is now two grade levels below expected level for age"

"Progress to . . ."

and progress are both relative and can be reporting variables (aspects of student performance that should be communicated about but not included directly in grades). The reference point for growth is the individual—one grows *from* where they were previously; the reference point for progress is competency—one progresses *to* or *toward* competency. Although it is critical for intrinsic motivation that students have a clear sense of their own growth and progress, grades must be measures of achievement *only* so that everyone knows what they mean.

Student Involvement

This is a critical area for student involvement. The better students understand the performance standards, both overall and at the task level, the more likely it is that they will achieve at a high level. Students therefore require opportunities to develop and use task-specific scoring tools containing age-appropriate, student-friendly descriptors of the meaning of the relevant summary symbols, so that they can accurately and usefully self-assess and set goals.

Summary

Grades are broken when any of the following occurs:

- When standards, continua, and levels are not clearly described.
- When standards, continua, and levels are not shared at the beginning of learning.
- When the achievement continua are unclear or inappropriate.
- When evidence is inaccurate.
- When the cutoff scores are arbitrary.
- When the level of proficiency required is unclear to graders or learners.
- When cutoffs vary profoundly across classrooms covering the same material.

The keys to success are thus as follows:

1. Overall and specific performance standards with a limited number of levels, clearly described in the language of the appropriate achievement continuum

2. Professional dialogue about performance standards between teachers, so they develop shared understanding and apply standards consistently

3. Clear, easily understandable student- and parent-friendly versions, made available from the beginning of instruction

> *Teacher Responsibilities for Performance Standards . . . engage in periodic moderation (group marking with other teachers using work samples, rubrics, and exemplars) to ensure collective agreement about the standards. (Cooper, 2007, p. 74)*

Teacher Vignette

Zach Fletcher, Palmyra School District, PA

As a speech and debate teacher, I recognize that grading students' "performances" could be very inconsistent. To help me be as consistent as possible in my grading, I give students rubrics before each of their major speeches. This not only keeps them informed of the areas of public speaking where they need to focus (nonverbal communication, vocal delivery, use of visual aids, etc.), but also focuses my assessment of their speeches. In this way, I hold them all to the same set of standards clearly defined at the onset. It sometimes takes us several days to get through a round of speeches. By holding students to clear descriptions of my expectations, I ensure that their grade is not a factor of my mood on a given day or how interesting I personally find their chosen topic.

Policy Example

El Monte City School District, CA

Draft Administrative Regulations

III. Academic Achievement

A. The Academic Achievement grade is an indicator of a student's mastery of grade-level Power Standards. Students demonstrate what they know, understand, and can do as measured through multiple assessments and observations.

4 *Exemplary* (exceeds)	3 *Proficient* (meets)	2 *Partially* *Proficient* (approaching)	1 *Non-Proficient* (below)

4 Exemplary: The student demonstrates mastery, with excellence, of the grade-level standards with relative ease and consistency, and often exceeds the cognitive level of the standards. The student applies and extends the key concepts, processes, and skills. The student is working at grade level yet at a higher level of Bloom's Taxonomy. There is no mark of 4+ or 4–.

3 Proficient: The student demonstrates mastery of the grade-level standards at the cognitive level the standard is written. The student consistently grasps and applies key concepts, processes, and skills with limited errors. There is no mark of 3+ or 3–.

2 Partially Proficient: The student demonstrates mastery of some grade-level standards. The student inconsistently grasps and applies some of the key concepts, processes, and skills with significant errors. There is no mark of 2+ or 2–.

1 Non-Proficient: The student has not demonstrated mastery of grade-level standards and is not yet performing at grade level. There is no mark of 1+ or 1–.

IV. Progress toward Proficiency

These marks represent the measurement of a student's growth toward and attainment of mastery of each district Power Standard in Reading, Writing, and Math. Progress is measured by a variety of evidence, which include quality standards-aligned assessments, portfolios, and other multiple measures.

√	∧	—	X
Meets Standard	Adequate Progress	Insufficient Progress	Standard Not Assessed

√   Meets or Exceeds Standard—The student has mastered the entire standard. Unless reassessment indicates otherwise, the √ is repeated in subsequent trimesters.

∧   Adequate Progress (Used 1st and 2nd Trimester only)—Based on what has been taught and assessed, the student is on track to master the standard by the end of the year. This symbol is not used third trimester.

—   Insufficient Progress—Based on what has been taught and assessed, the student has not demonstrated that s/he is on track to master the standard by the end of the year. For third trimester, this symbol represents that the student has NOT demonstrated mastery of the standard in its entirety.

X   Standard Not Assessed (Used 1st and 2nd Trimester only)—Standard has not been taught and/or measured to date. This symbol is not used third trimester.

Fix 9

Don't assign grades based on a student's achievement compared to other students; compare each student's performance to preset standards.

Grading on the curve makes learning a highly competitive activity in which students compete against one another for the few scarce rewards (high grades) distributed by the teacher. Under these conditions, students readily see that helping others become successful threatens their own chances for success. As a result, learning becomes a game of winners and losers; and because the number of rewards is kept arbitrarily small, most students are forced to be losers.

—Guskey, 1996a, pp. 18–19

Grades are broken when they compare students to each other. The fix is to base grades on preset achievement standards—to be criterion referenced, not norm referenced in assigning grades. In doing so, we acknowledge that it is possible for all students to get an A or for all students to get an F. There would be no plan to intentionally distribute grades on a construct such as the bell curve, ensuring a few A's, more B's, even more C's, some D's and a few F's.

You can test the thinking in your school or district by asking this question: "What do you think would happen if you did an outstanding job, all the students in your class did an outstanding job, and all the students received an A?" If the response is that the grades would be questioned with comments such as, "easy teacher," "no or low standards," or "grade inflation," then you are in a norm-referenced setting. If on the other hand the grades were questioned but the comments were "great," "that's what we want," or "let's celebrate lots of winners," you are in a criterion-referenced setting.

One of the main problems in assigning grades based on student-to-student comparisons is, What should be the reference group? Should an individual student be compared to others in their particular class at that time? All who have taken that class over time? From their particular teacher or from all teachers? What span of "all teachers"? Because there is no easy answer, interpretation of and communication with such grades is difficult at best and impossible at worst.

The rationale often cited for creating a competitive grading environment in standards-driven schools is that it provides motivation for students and that highly motivated students learn more. In fact, however, the motivational effects are not beneficial for all students. Students who finish high in the ranking and therefore have hope of getting good grades may indeed be motivated. For those at the bottom, motivation wanes. They set lower standards for themselves in order to maintain their personal sense of self-worth, and put forth only the effort required to meet those adjusted standards. Competitive grading systems do not reward such students, who are often "left behind" their peers both in school and beyond.

Summary

Grading students by comparing their performance to one another distorts individual achievement. We need clear, criterion-referenced achievement standards—absolute, *not* relative, standards that describe a limited number of levels: at, below, and above proficiency. Teachers in a noncompetitive grading system assign grades to each student based *only* on that student's own achievement in relation to the applicable standards.

There are a very few legitimate uses for norm-referenc(ing) . . . in school, and all of them are where students are competing for limited resources. (Brookhart, 2004, p. 73)

Teacher Vignettes

Cristina C. Rathyen, Moanalua High School, Honolulu, HI

I use a criterion-referenced final exam for both AP literature and Honors Literature. It's a take-home test that allows students time to think about how they want to demonstrate their learning. There is no bell curve and everyone can earn an A if they demonstrate that they have read deeply and thoughtfully. They are allowed to bring all their materials and notes to the exam, but the actual essay must be written in class, either on the computer or by hand. They may bring with them an outline and a thesis statement for this essay. I have had very good luck with this method and students are usually given one class period to work together on their topics and do some of the requisite research. Most students achieve very well on this test, and the essays are fun to read.

Policy Example

Halifax Regional School Board Assessment, Evaluation and Communication of Student Learning Policy (Revised September 24, 2008)

6.3 Grades and report cards will be based solely upon individual learning and will accurately reflect achievement of the outcomes as defined by the provincial curriculum and/or individual program plan. As such, individual student achievement will:
    6.3.1 Be measured against defined curriculum outcomes rather than compared to other students or measures of individual academic growth.

Don't rely on evidence gathered using assessments that fail to meet standards of quality; rely only on quality assessments.

Quality classroom assessment produces accurate information that is used effectively to maximize student learning.

—Stiggins et al., 2004, p. 26

G rades are broken when the evidence used is from poor-quality assessment and so misrepresents student achievement. This is the classic "garbage in, garbage out" syndrome. The fix is to have clear standards of assessment quality and to apply these standards to each and every assessment.

Figure 3.8 provides a framework of standards for ensuring high-quality assessment. Quality assessment requires that we have accurate assessment that is effectively used. Accurate assessment, the focus of this Fix, requires that we pay attention to three questions: Why are we assessing? What are we assessing? How will we assess it? The purpose of each assessment must be clear. In the context of this book, the assessment must be for grading purposes—an assessment *of* learning. The learning goals to be assessed are those established standards students are to master, specifying both what is expected and how well students must perform to earn each grade.

Figure 3.8 The Keys to Quality Classroom Assessment

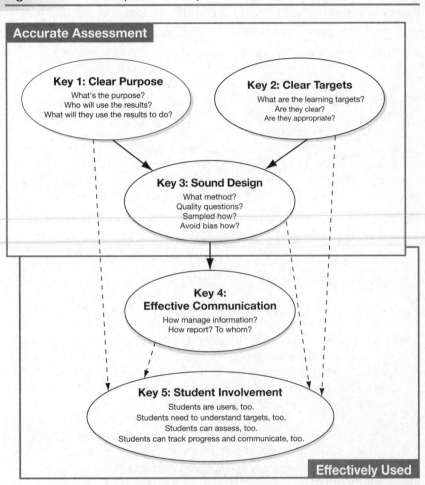

Source: From *Classroom Assessment for Student Learning: Doing It Right—Using It Well* (p. 302) by R. J. Stiggins, J. A. Arter, J. Chappuis, and S. Chappuis, 2004, Portland, OR: Assessment Training Institute. Copyright © 2010, 2006, 2004 by Pearson. Reprinted by permission of Pearson.

(Students therefore must have these learning targets available and must understand them clearly.) We address the matter of how we will assess by considering the following features of design quality in creating assessments for use in grading:

1. Use a proper assessment method for the context; that is, a method that will effectively and efficiently gather the needed evidence of student achievement. The proper method depends on the nature of the learning goals. For example, to assess student mastery of content knowledge, we can rely on selected response or essay formats. But to assess mastery of performance skills or the ability to create products that meet certain standards of quality, we must turn to performance assessment.

2. Build assessments out of high-quality ingredients. If the test is to rely on multiple-choice items, they must be *good* items, not bad ones. Performance assessments must be built of high-quality exercises and rubrics. Classroom assessors must know and understand the differences.

3. Sample student achievement appropriately; that is, gather enough evidence to make valid and reliable judgments of proficiency gained in relation to grade expectations. We know we have enough evidence when we can confidently say that, if we gathered one more item, it would simply confirm what we know now. There is a base or minimum amount of evidence needed from every student, but that amount will not be the same for each student. The more consistent a student is, the less evidence is needed; the more inconsistent, the more evidence is needed. This is just one of several factors that teachers might take into account in deciding how to sample student achievement for grading and how samples might vary across students. (For more detail see Stiggins et al., 2004.)

4. Avoid bias that can distort results. There can be problems with the student, the assessment setting, the scoring process, or the assessment itself that can cause the score to misrepresent student achievement. Problems that can occur with the student include lack of reading skill, emotional upset, poor health, lack of testwiseness, and evaluation anxiety. Problems within the setting that can distract student attention include heat, noise,

and lack of light. Problems in scoring include inter-rater dis-agreement on criteria. Problems that can occur with the assessment include insufficient time for all students to complete the assessment.*

It is well worth noting here, too, that Black and Wiliam (1998) and others have documented that high-quality, accurate classroom assessments in and of themselves measurably improve student learning. This alone is a potent reason—and perhaps the best reason—to strive to ensure that our assessments meet the highest standards of quality and accuracy.

Summary

Grades are broken when they arise from poor-quality assessment, because the evidence is not accurate. The fix is to check every assessment for quality—clear purpose, clear learning goals, sound design, and avoidance of bias. Assessments that do not meet these four standards of quality will mismeasure student achievement and thus will lead to inaccurate grades.

> *Evaluation experts stress that if you are going to make important decisions about students that have broad implication, such as decisions involved in grading, then you must have good evidence. . . . In the absence of good evidence, even the most detailed grading and reporting system is useless. (Guskey & Bailey, 2001, p. 46, as quoted in Butler & McMunn, 2006, p. 188)*

---

* "Few tasks in life—and very few tasks in scholarship—actually depend on being able to read passages or solve math problems rapidly. As a teacher, I want my students to read, write and think well; I don't care how much time they spend on their assignments. For those few jobs where speed is important, timed tests may be useful" (Gardner, 2002, n.p.).

Teacher Vignette

Mike Fryda, Westside High School, Westside Community Schools, Omaha, NE

I reached a pivotal moment in my career in which I recognized that assessment quality was a serious problem for me. Since that realization I went back to the classroom myself, improved my assessment writing skills, and received a second endorsement in Assessment Leadership K–12. While working on my graduate work, I learned a lot about how educators approach evidence for learning.

Most educators have been taught that sound assessment practices involve getting the maximum number of measurements of student learning so that we can get an accurate measurement of what they actually know and can do. Rarely does the conversation talk about the quality of those assessments. It is difficult for many educators to believe that they can assess and grade less if they improve the quality of their assessments. I think part of this is due to the fact that many teachers assess the way they were assessed in school. The problem is that the way they were assessed in school may not have been adequate to begin with, and they received little instruction on assessment in teacher preparation programs. If a student fails the test, it is the student's fault, not the teacher's fault.

When I evaluate an assessment I ask myself three questions that guide how I make changes.

The first question I always ask myself is if the assessment format is the appropriate format for what we are trying to assess. Written response assessments, while more time consuming, will always be a better measure of higher-order thinking than multiple-choice tests. That doesn't mean that it isn't possible to write a multiple-choice test directed at higher-order thinking. Writing is a much more accurate evaluation, although it takes more time to develop and score.

The second question I ask myself is: How many *quality* items do I really need to get a good judgment of what a student knows about an idea? The best practice convention is six to eight items per broad content standard. This is a big assessment misconception. Those numbers get thrown around frequently, but when teachers assimilate those numbers into their philosophy of "more is better" the end result is overassessing. A 40-question unit test on one broad standard is overkill. What tends to happen in my experience is that students get so overwhelmed by the sheer size of the test that their ability to think thoughtfully about the items diminishes. My tests are composed of 10–12 high-quality multiple-choice questions that follow all the conventions of multiple-choice items designed to pinpoint where the errors are in student understanding. A teacher can do more to assess student understanding with 10 well-written items than they can with 40 that are poorly written.

The final question I ask myself in reviewing the quality of assessments in my class is to ask: How many times have I summatively assessed students on a standard? The goal is to always assess them *once*, near the end of the practice period. There is no reason to summatively assess a student when they are beginning with their understanding, again when they are progressing and again when they are proficient. That distorts their final achievement. We want to assess them for a grade only after they have had every opportunity to understand.

Crafting sound assessments is an incredibly difficult task. Tackling this task has really helped us to be more efficient in assessing kids. We have seen decreases in the amount of late and missing work simply because we are not flooding students with unnecessary repetition. We spend that time in having higher-quality practice so that when students see a summative assessment of a section, it is not overwhelming. Students have also been less frustrated on summative assessments because we have worked hard to make them efficient measures of what students understand, not questions intended to trick, or high volumes of superficial knowledge-based questions.

Policy Example

Bremerton School District, WA

7. **Grades are determined based on evidence.**
   Grades are determined based on evidence from accurate assessments, some of which are common assessments.
   a. Accuracy requires:
      i. appropriate and clear targets derived from state standards
      ii. sound design, which would include:
         1. appropriate methods (assessment strategies that match learning goals. For example: knowledge learning goals may be assessed with selected response but skill learning goals must be assessed with performance assessments)
         2. well-written tasks and items
         3. appropriate sampling (sufficient items on each learning goal/concept tested and sufficient evidence for each learning goal/concept over a period of time)
         4. avoidance of bias
   b. Summative assessments
      i. Content area classes/courses should include a combination of class-/teacher-specific assessments and collaboratively selected common assessments. Each department and grade level should determine the appropriate ratio of each type of assessment.
      ii. Teachers are encouraged to develop common summative assessments collaboratively.

Chapter 4

Fixes for Inappropriate Grade Calculation

Fixes

11 Don't rely only on the mean; consider other measures of central tendency and use professional judgment.

12 Don't include zeros in grade determination when evidence is missing or as punishment; use alternatives, such as reassessing to determine real achievement, or use "I" for Incomplete or Insufficient Evidence.

Fix 11

Don't rely only on the mean; consider other measures of central tendency and use professional judgment.

Educators must abandon the average, or arithmetic mean, as the predominant measurement of student achievement.

—Reeves, 2000, p. 10, emphasis added

Grades are broken when the summary they provide of student achievement is inaccurate because the procedures used to arrive at the grade are faulty. For example, grades may mislead when they are based on simply calculating the mean (average) of a series of scores, due to the effect of outlier scores. The fix for grades broken in this way is to not use the mean as "the measure" by considering other measures of central tendency, and to recognize that grading should not be merely a numerical, mechanical exercise.

The problem with the mean is well illustrated in this quote from a letter to the editor in one of my local newspapers:

> Whenever I hear statistics being quoted I am reminded of the statistician who drowned while wading across a river with an average depth of three feet. (McMann, 2003, n.p.)

The mean can be very well named—it is truly "mean" to students because it overemphasizes outlier scores, which are most often low outliers. As we see in the following case, the calculation of the mean can distort the final grade. Ten assessments have been converted to percentage scores to calculate a final grade:

$$91, 91, 91, 91, 91, 91, 91, 70, 91, 91$$
$$\text{Total} = 889, \text{Mean} = 88.9, \text{Final grade} = B$$

This student performed at an A level 9 times out of 10 and the 70 is clearly an anomaly. But the grade as calculated in most schools would be a B. This example raises both a general issue—How should evidence be summarized?; and one derived from it—Should evidence be summarized by strict mathematical calculation?

Somewhat ironically, in most states and provinces, somewhere about Grade 6 students are taught in Math class about three methods of calculating central tendency—mean, median, and mode. They are taught that each measure of central tendency has both virtues and problems, and that, depending on the distribution of scores and your purpose, you carefully choose the appropriate measure for every situation. But somehow teachers frequently ignore this in managing their own gradebooks. If students are very consistent each measure will get the same result and the mean can suffice. But the more inconsistent a student's performance is the less effective any of the measures of central tendency is in accurately summarizing student achievement. Guskey, addressing the issue of summarizing when the record includes extreme scores, notes that "averaging falls far short of providing an accurate description of what students have learned. . . . If the purpose of grading and reporting is to provide an accurate description of what students have learned, then *averaging* must be considered *inadequate* and *inappropriate*" (Guskey, 1996a, p. 21, emphasis added).

So if the mean is "inadequate and inappropriate," what number crunching should be done? The median (middle score by rank) or the mode (the most frequently occurring score) are generally more appropriate than the mean when confronted with extreme scores. Russell Wright has written extensively about the use of the median, arguing that "grading by the median provides more opportunities for success by diminishing the impact of a few stumbles and by rewarding hard work [what I would call *consistency*]" (Wright, 1994, p. 723). In the previous example, if the median or the mode is used, the student would get their deserved A. It is necessary then for teachers to consider all measures of central tendency when determining grades.

At this point we have to ask, "Should grades in fact be determined by straight mathematical computation only?" Given the limitations of measures of central tendency to deal effectively with all score distributions and the many factors affecting student performance I conclude that we have to see grading not as simply a numerical, mechanical exercise, but *primarily* as an exercise in professional judgment. It calls for teachers to demonstrate two key aspects of professional behavior—the application of craft knowledge of sound assessment practice and the willingness and ability to make and be ready to defend one's professional judgment. As teachers we must ask the question, "Based on all the evidence of achievement a student has produced, which summary symbol most accurately represents that achievement?" That is why I always talk about "determining," not "calculating" grades—number crunching may be necessary but ultimately grading requires professional judgment. Each teacher must be prepared to specify: "These were my expectations, here is the evidence of each student's mastery of them. Using the following summary process, here is the grade I determined for each student. . . ." In borderline cases, teachers may allow or encourage students to present additional evidence to persuade the teacher to judge their achievement more accurately.

An example of a teacher determining grades by combining number crunching with her professional judgment is illustrated in the following: "I thought your talk at Bronxville was very thought provoking and as I went over my grades for the year over the weekend I was thinking all the time of things you had made us consider. I definitely have a number of students for whom I will reject the average. I feel liberated!! Thanks" (anonymous personal communication, June 2002). The writer went on to say that for 100 of her 105 mostly very high-achieving students the mean was an accurate representation of their achievement, but for 5 students it wasn't and for those 5 she used her professional judgment.

Summary

Grades are frequently broken (inaccurate) when they result only from the calculation of the mean in contexts where extreme scores distort; they can be repaired by considering other measures of central tendency and using professional judgment. Thus we should think and talk about not the calculation, but the *determination* of grades.

> *Not everything that can be counted counts, and not everything that counts can be counted. (Albert Einstein, quoted in ASCD SmartBrief, 19 December 2001, n.p.)*

Teacher Vignette

Trevor Metz and Jamie Thompson, Caesar Rodney School District, DE

We use more than just averages in determining grades. We use other measures of central tendency; median, mode. After attending training we realized that often we use the average because that is the norm. Using total points or weighting categories is how most of us were graded in school and, in our case, how we in turn graded our students. Soon after we began looking at other measures and using what is appropriate for students. We override and we're proud of it! When a student retakes an assignment we override the original score with the new. Our grading software allows us to enter a comment with each grade. Here we record the original score to help keep track of improvement/regression. At interims and the end of the marking period we review student performance before grades are submitted. Is one grade from one bad day bringing down the average? If so, we look at the mode, for example, as a better measure of progress towards the standards. Is there additional evidence that understanding improved as we moved through the content? If the answer is yes, then we incorporate that evidence into our final determination and override. It feels good to override grades and know that we are communicating accurate performance to student and parents.

Policy Example

Grand Island Public Schools, NE

Guideline 7: Use care when crunching scores to determine grades.

- When determining grades, consider the body of evidence and use professional judgment. Don't just calculate grades
- When averaging scores, serious consideration should be given to using the median or mode. When possible avoid using the mean.

Rationale

The median, which is the middle score in a group of scores is (frequently) a far more encouraging way of calculating grades. The commonly used mean or average calculation tends to emphasize lower (outlier) scores. Often the median is statistically accurate while the mean is not. Consideration should also be given to the use of the mode, which is the most frequently occurring score or level.

Fix 12

Don't include zeros in grade determination when evidence is missing or as punishment; use alternatives, such as reassessing to determine real achievement, or use "I" for Incomplete or Insufficient Evidence.

Most state standards in mathematics require that fifth-grade students understand the principles of ratios—for example, A is to B as 4 is to 3; D is to F as 1 is to zero. Yet the persistence of the zero on the 100-point scale indicates that many people with advanced degrees . . . have not applied the ratio standard to their own professional practices.

—*Reeves, 2004, pp. 324–325*

Grades are broken when zeros are entered into a student's academic record for missing evidence or as punishment for transgressions. When combined with other evidence, the resulting grade does not accurately reflect student achievement. There are several fixes for the use of zeros in grades—by far the best is the use of "I" as a final grade, indicating Incomplete or Insufficient Evidence, but as transitional approaches or in situations where calculation "rules," acceptable alternatives are the use of equal difference scales or the use of a "floor" score that makes a percentage scale an equal difference scale.

Zeros most commonly are found in teachers' gradebooks when students fail to submit required assessment evidence, such as turning in assignments. They are also sometimes used for serious behavioral infractions such as cheating. There are three fundamental problems with zeros:

- Zeros give a numerical value to something that has never been assessed, and therefore has no basis in reality.
- They can have counterproductive effects on student motivation.
- They involve inappropriate mathematics.

But the most important issue is that zeros in the record render grades ineffective as communication because the resulting grade is an inaccurate representation of the student's achievement.

Assigning a zero to something that has not been seen compromises the accuracy of the grade and does so to an unknown extent. Such misinformation can only lead to poor-quality decisions about students and their learning.

Regarding motivation, as soon as students have more than one zero they have little chance of recovery, increasing the likelihood that they will give up. In high school for some students this can happen as early as the end of the first month of the school year, effectively rendering the remainder of the year a waste of time, at least from a learning perspective. One potential side effect is that students who have given up often have discipline problems. The other motivational problem is that students who are not concerned about grades are willing to "take a zero" and are thus not held accountable for their learning. We are faced with the irony that a policy that may be grounded in the belief of holding students accountable (giving zeros) actually allows some students to escape accountability for learning.

The mathematical problem with zeros is that they represent very extreme scores and their effect on the grade is always exaggerated. As we have established, this is not acceptable.

The best alternative to the use of zeros is the use of an "I" for Incomplete or Insufficient Evidence. When desired evidence of student achievement is missing, teachers decide whether they have sufficient evidence to determine a grade and if they do not, assign an "I." Guskey and Bailey suggest that this "is both educationally sound and potentially quite effective" (2001, p. 144). One reason is that it clearly places the responsibility where it should be—with the student. It is the student's responsibility to produce sufficient (but not necessarily all) evidence required so the teacher can make a valid summary judgment. It is extremely important that schools/districts have this option available to teachers on each report of student achievement, including the final report card. The "I" has the same impact as an F (in high school = no credit), but it accurately communicates what the problem is. Another benefit is that while zeros can doom students to failure very early in the school year, with support and time an Incomplete can most often be made complete (sufficient). Schools/districts need to have clear procedures and timelines for students to move from an "I" to a grade that accurately represents their achievement. This is the positive, supportive approach that is likely to be much more effective in promoting further learning than is the negative and punitive impact of zeros.

For consistency across each school, the specific policy adopted should be developed at the school/district level. Teachers may then apply the policy in the manner best fitting their classrooms. Given that many schools/districts are still in transition to a full standards-based approach and still have grading policies that require calculation (often including the use of percentage scales), we also must consider alternatives to zeros in those situations.

Zeros are generally used in grading scales that have unequal differences in the points on the scale so that an included zero has a disproportionate effect. The most commonly used grading scale is A = 90–100 percent, B = 80–89, C = 70–79, D = 60–69, and F = below 60 percent. In this scale there are 11 points for an A, 10 for each of B, C, and D, and 60 points for an F. The problem with using this scale, and three possible solutions, are illustrated in Table 4.1. This student was supposed to do five assessments but does only four; his scores are A, B, C, and D (represented by midpoint percentage

Table 4.1 Alternatives to Zeros

			Equal Difference Scales	
	Scores	101-Point Scale	5-Point Scale	50-Point Scale
	95	90–100 (A)	4	95
	85	80–89 (B)	3	85
	75	70–79 (C)	2	75
	65	60–69 (D)	1	65
	0	<60 (F)	0	50
Mean	64 (D)		2 (C)	74 (C)
Median	75 (C)		2 (C)	75 (C)

scores in Column 1) on the four assessments and a zero for the assessment he does not submit. The mean for the four assessments he did is 80 percent—a B, but the zero lowers the mean to 64 percent—a grade of D, a drastic reduction caused by the range for an F being approximately six times greater than the range for the other grades (Column 2). Alternatives appear in Columns 3 and 4 (Equal Difference Scales) and in the bottom row (Median). Using the 5-point scale in Column 3 results in a summary grade of C; this is still lower than the mean of this student's scores but is a more reasonable summary of his achievement. Column 4 turns the percentage scale into an equal difference scale by having (almost) the same number of points for each grade level, using a floor of 50 percent. (Instead of recording a zero for missing evidence the teacher would record a score of 50 percent. This symbolic percentage is chosen to equalize the points per grade; it does not mean that students have mastered 50 percent of what is expected; it means that if students actually attempt an assessment and receive a failing percentage grade it must be recorded as a percentage between 50 and 59.) The third alternative appears in the bottom row—use the median instead of the mean. Note that each alternative results in a grade of C. (For further information about alternatives to zeros see Guskey, 2005.)

Table 4.2 illustrates the need for more than simply numerical alternatives to the use of zeros. In this example, none of the measures of central tendency provide sufficient accuracy. Students were expected to submit 10 assessments. This student submitted only 3, receiving scores of 95, 85, and 80 percent. A zero was assigned for each of her missing assignments. If the traditional percentage scale is used, she would receive a failing grade. But the 3 assessments that were submitted clearly indicate that she had a good understanding of the material assessed. If an equal difference scale such as the 5-point scale in Table 4.1 is used, she receives a passing grade, but it is unlikely that she provided sufficient evidence if she only did 3 of 10 required assessments. Also, such an approach would support the undesirable idea that students can pick which assessments they do and choose to take a zero on other assessments. Thus there is

Table 4.2   The Impact of Zeros

	101-Point Scale	*5-Point Scale*
	95	4
	0	0
	0	0
	0	0
	85	3
	0	0
	0	0
	80	3
	0	0
	0	0
Total	260	10
Mean	26	1.0
Median	0	0
Letter Grade	F	D

a problem with both scales, and the median is clearly not helpful in this situation because it would be zero. This student's appropriate grade would be an "I" for Incomplete or Insufficient Evidence, because it most clearly communicates the problem without distorting her actual achievement.

Another approach to controlling the use of zeros in high schools and middle schools is to use sampling to eliminate the need for them. This starts with developing and announcing assessment plans that identify the learning targets to be mastered, and that specify in advance the summative assessments that will provide the necessary evidence (both what will be assessed and when). The teachers then build overlapping assessments, each replicating part of the evidence provided by the previous one. As long as students complete a reasonable number of the assessments, a sufficient sample of the learning goals is achieved, and they will have produced enough evidence for the determination of a grade. Students who do not complete enough assessments will receive an "I" for Insufficient Evidence, which will remain until they submit sufficient evidence.

Student Involvement

When students understand the impact of not submitting required assessment evidence, and know what alternatives are in place in their school, they are better able to decide about submitting needed academic evidence and/or making up an Incomplete. Support sessions may be available before or after school or at lunchtime in which they could participate. Students also can be involved in determining the consequences for failure to submit required assessment evidence. For example, they may agree to a contract that requires them to meet certain timelines and/or to attend specific support sessions.

Student-led conferences also may help students recognize their responsibilities, by helping them identify both their strengths and areas needing improvement. Dyck (2002) tells how one student-led conference helped a student to identify his problem with missing assignments, and also helped him recognize his successes (including an excellent PowerPoint presentation). Dyck notes that "at the end of the conference Greg left with two proud parents and a plan for finishing those delinquent assignments" (p. 41).

Summary

Grades are broken when zeros are used; zeros distort the actual achievement record and can decrease student motivation to learn. There are, however, many fixes in the form of grading alternatives. Schools/districts develop policies regarding these alternatives, then indicate to their teachers which alternative(s) they can or should use in their classrooms. Support for this approach has been acknowledged in Canada at the provincial level in a major review of assessment practices in Alberta: "On occasion, teachers unintentionally engage in unfair assessment practice. For example, when teachers award a student a zero for work not handed in on time, they fail to acknowledge that, first, the zero is not an accurate description of achievement or of students' understanding of content material, but instead behavior, and second, one zero averaged with other grades has a devastating effect on a student's overall grade, particularly if the work that was assigned a zero has been heavily weighted" (Webber, Aitken, Lupart, & Scott, 2009, p. 7).

> *A zero has an undeserved and devastating influence, so much so that no matter what the student does, the grade distorts the final grade as a true indicator of mastery. Mathematically and ethically this is unacceptable. (Wormeli, 2006, pp. 137–138)*

Teacher Vignette

Myron Dueck, Summerland School District, BC

Brett was a senior in my twentieth-century history class at the time that I switched away from giving zeros and rather assigned the term "INCOMPLETE" to work that was missing. Once a student had one missing assignment, I did not calculate an overall score until the work was submitted, as my argument was, "How can I assign a cumulative score when a component is missing?" It was like awarding a final time in a triathlon before the final run was complete.

It turned out that Brett was missing a major assignment and therefore when he went to check his course standing on the printout I had posted at the back of the room, he was disappointed to discover he was simply listed as 'INCOMPLETE." Brett approached me on this issue.

"So, Mr. Dueck, I was wondering what my grade was in the course at the moment."

"I suppose we could guess on it Brett, but until I get your missing assignment in, it will be very hard to tell."

"Why don't you just put in a zero and let's see where I am at?"

"Sorry Brett, I can't give a zero for something I never saw."

"C'mon, just put in a zero and we'll call it even."

"Nope."

"So if I hand it in late, is it true that you do not take off late marks?"

"You can check your course outline—I do not deduct for late assignments."

"Alright, I will give it some thought and I will most likely bring the assignment in."

Two days later Brett delivered his Paris Peace Conference project and he had done quite a good job on it.

I was a little curious, and so I asked Brett why he had delivered a good project when just a few days earlier he had asked if he could just get a zero. I wondered why he hadn't done the bare minimum.

"Well, I had a really crazy week and a lot of stuff on the go. Knowing I could still do well, made me still try to get it done. More than anything though, it was that INC on my grade that made the difference."

I asked, "What's the big deal about the INC?"

"It's all about the anticipation and suspense. I mean, I get up from my desk, walk over to the grade sheet, and look up my number. I then glance across my individual grades and all the while the anticipation is building to see my final score. Much to my dismay, when I get to the end, I see an INC rather than a mark. That is really . . . irksome."

"So, would you have preferred a zero?"

"No, but with a zero, I probably wouldn't have bothered getting it done."

"Hang on Brett, help me out here . . . you care about your grades, you obviously know a lot about the course, I would imagine the threat of a zero would make you get it done."

"It's zero, it brings my grade down, but it is not a big deal. Zero is a punishment, not a motivator. Punishment has never really motivated me. A chance to improve my mark, or in this case to change from an INC, now that is motivating . . . at least from my perspective. Any other questions, Mr. Dueck?"

"Nope."

"Have a nice day."

Policy Example

Bremerton School District, WA

9. Missing Evidence of Learning

An Incomplete ("I") will be used when a student has not submitted required evidence of learning.

   a. Assignments that have not been submitted by the due date should be recorded as "NS" (not submitted) and not recorded as zeros. The conditions for completing a missing assignment must be established between the teacher and the student and it is the student's responsibility to meet those conditions.

   b. When there is insufficient evidence of learning to report a semester grade an Incomplete ("I") will be used for reporting student achievement.

c. If an "I" is used for a semester report, a student has up to 75
    school days of the following semester to submit the required
    evidence of student learning to convert the "I" to a grade. It is
    the student's responsibility to submit the required evidence to the
    teacher or department chair. If inadequate evidence is submitted,
    then the "I" remains on the student transcript and no credit is
    given for the course.

Chapter 5

Fixes to Support Learning

Fixes

13 Don't use information from formative assessments and practice to determine grades; use only summative evidence.

14 Don't summarize evidence accumulated over time when learning is developmental and will grow with time and repeated opportunities; in those instances, emphasize more recent achievement.

15 Don't leave students out of the grading process. Involve students; they can—and should—play key roles in assessment and grading that promote achievement.

Fix 13

Don't use information from formative assessments and practice to determine grades; use only summative evidence.

The primary responsibility of our school is teaching and learning.

The individuality of every learner is recognized and welcomed.

The school culture nurtures both the joy of learning and the satisfaction of achievement.

Our shared vision of education empowers us to explore, experiment and grow.

Learners accept responsibility for their own learning . . .

— *School District of Clayton, MO, 2003, n.p.*

Grades are broken if scores for everything students do find their way into report card grades. The fix is to include, in all but specific, limited cases, only evidence from summative assessments intended to document learning, that is, designed to serve as assessments *of* learning.

The primary purpose of grades is to communicate a summary of student achievement at a particular point in time; that is, what students know, understand, and can do as a result of their learning. It is important that teachers, students, and parents recognize that *learning* is a process in which learners increase their knowledge, understanding, and skills as a result of effort, instruction, feedback from teachers and peers, and self-assessment and adjustment. As Jay

McTighe points out, "We know that students will rarely perform at high levels on challenging learning tasks at their first attempt. Deep understanding or high levels of proficiency are achieved only as a result of trial, practice, adjustments based on feedback, and more practice" (McTighe, 1996–1997, p. 11). For this process to work well learners must believe that it is important and worthwhile to try and that it is acceptable to take risks and make mistakes; it is not necessary to always "get it" the first time.

This process is clearly acknowledged in the guiding principles of the School District of Clayton, Missouri, given in the opening quotation. However, it is not recognized when teachers include in grades evidence generated during practice (i.e., learning) activities. Unfortunately, this happens daily in many classrooms, when teachers judge everything students do and then use every piece of evidence to determine grades.

Standards-based teachers distinguish clearly between teaching activities (which include diagnostic and formative assessment) through which students learn and practice, and summative assessments, when students "perform" and show what they know, understand, and can do (Figure 5.1). They are clear about the purpose

Figure 5.1 Purposes of Assessment

Diagnostic—assessment that takes place prior to instruction; designed to determine a student's attitude, skills or knowledge in order to identify student needs.

Formative—assessment designed to provide direction for improvement and/or adjustment to a program for individual students or for a whole class, e.g. observation, quizzes, homework (usually), instructional questions, initial drafts/attempts. (*Assessments FOR learning*)

Summative—assessment designed to provide information to be used in making judgments about a student's achievement at the end of a sequence of instruction, e.g. final drafts/attempts, tests, exams, assignments, projects, performances. (*Assessments OF learning*)

of every activity, and include directly in grades *only* evidence from summative assessments. This view is emphasized and described clearly by three Michigan middle school teachers in the April 2010 *Phi Delta Kappan* (Deddeh, Main, & Ratzlaff Fulkerson, 2010).

It is critical that both teachers and students recognize when assessment is primarily *for* learning (formative) and when it is primarily *of* learning (summative). Students understand this in band and sports, when practice is clearly identified and separate from an actual performance or game. But often this is not clear in the classroom. If we did in basketball what we frequently do in the classroom the game would not start 0–0, but each team would start with a score based on an assessment of the quality of their practices in the days leading up to the game. Obviously this would be absurd—and it is equally so in the classroom.

A large and growing body of research supports this distinction. The Assessment Reform Group in the United Kingdom, which sponsored "Inside the Black Box," the important paper by Paul Black and Dylan Wiliam (Black & Wiliam, 1998), has commissioned and published much of this research. "Firm evidence shows that formative assessment is an essential component of classroom work and that its development can raise standards of achievement, Mr. Black and Mr. Wiliam point out. Indeed, they know of no other way of raising standards for which such a strong prima facie case can be made" (editor's introduction to Black & Wiliam, 1998, p. 139). Their research and the work of others have shown that improving formative assessment and using assessment *for* learning raises the achievement of all students, but also that it has the most significant impact on low achievers. Learning gains made through using assessment *for* learning are similar to those achieved through one-on-one coaching.

The key components of assessment *for* learning are (1) sharing the learning target(s) with students from the beginning of the learning, (2) making adjustments in teaching as a result of formative assessment, (3) providing descriptive feedback to students from assessment, and (4) providing opportunities for students to self- and peer assess so that they understand their strengths and what they need to do to improve. This is obviously very different from a summative use of assessment—from putting a score or number on everything students do and including every bit of evidence when computing grades. Such summative assessment is important, but only when balanced with appropriate formative assessments. Students should be assessed regularly; everything (or almost everything) they do can be assessed and/or checked, but everything does not need a score and every score need not be included in the grade. Some student work must be for practice only, and be returned to them accompanied by the kind of feedback that will help them do better the next time.

Black and Wiliam define *formative assessment* as "all those activities undertaken by teachers and by their students [that] provide information to be used as feedback to modify the teaching and learning activities in which they are engaged" (Black & Wiliam, 1998, p. 139). To appropriately modify learning, feedback has to be effective; it has to be timely, describe features of the work or performance relating directly to learning targets and/or standards of quality; and be low stakes—i.e., allow for adjustments before it "counts." This means that feedback has to be descriptive, not evaluative. A 7/10 or a 3 (from a rubric) going into a gradebook is high stakes, provides no useful information about the learning targets, and contributes nothing that will improve learning. One of the important implications of this is that teachers need to identify clearly and record evidence derived from formative assessment separately from evidence from summative assessment. This can be done using separate pages for each in the gradebook, by color-coding entries, or by giving a zero weight to formative assessments in a computerized gradebook or spreadsheet.

One of the most common practices in North American education has been scoring and including all homework as a significant part of grades. This has been done in the belief that it promotes responsibility in students, but in fact it often has the opposite effect. Careful consideration has to be given to the purpose(s) of homework. Sometimes homework requires students to show what they know by extending or integrating their knowledge and understanding through projects or assignments done partially or completely outside the classroom. This is clearly summative assessment and is legitimately part of grades as long as there is careful monitoring to ensure that it is the student's own work. Another purpose for homework is preparation—introducing knowledge, understanding, and skills intended to help students to be ready for subsequent lessons. As this happens *before* instruction any assessment would be diagnostic, which obviously has no place in grades. Most often, however, homework is practice of whatever was learned in class that day—any assessment of this work should be regarded as formative. Practice is valuable only to those students who can have some degree of success on their own without teacher support. It is of little or no value to students that don't need to practice, and it can actually be damaging to students who don't understand because they may embed misunderstandings that will be difficult to correct.

Putting a mark on work done for practice renders it effectively summative, not formative. When homework assigned as practice is scored and included in grades, what becomes most important to students is that it be done because it "counts," not because of any learning that might occur. It becomes an issue of compliance so it really doesn't matter who does the homework—the student, a parent, a sibling, or a friend. If we want homework to be about learning, we need students to understand that it is for practice if they need it, not compliance or grading, because then the person who benefits from the homework is the learner.

One major concern that is often expressed about not including practice homework in grades is, "Students won't do their homework if I don't grade it!" We have done an absolutely superb job of training students into this perspective by putting a number on everything they do and making every number part of the grade. But as we have trained them into it, we can train them out of it. The motivation for practicing and doing homework should come from each student's clear understanding that it will contribute to their learning. We want them to feel a sense of satisfaction from knowing, understanding, or being able to do something better today than yesterday. We want them to come to understand, "If I had done my homework, I would have done better on the test." We can tell them this day after day with no effect, but when they see the assessment evidence speak for itself and understand that practice really does help, they will come to this realization themselves.

As stated, including practice homework in grades can be damaging to struggling students because they may develop misunderstandings that will be difficult to correct. It is also damaging to these students because it reduces their willingness to try. If they know that they are going to get a low score, then to avoid yet another failure one defense mechanism is not to do it. It is better to keep the stakes low and have students understand, "It is okay to try because if I try I am going to get feedback on what I did well and what needs improvement."

Including practice homework in grades can also be damaging in other ways. Consider this quote from Elinor Burkett, after spending a year observing in a suburban Minneapolis high school: "Nick was fed up; . . . fed up with acing exams but getting C's at the end of the trimester because he refused to do the worksheets assigned in order to help students study so they could ace exams" (Burkett, 2002, p. 124). Nick did not need to do the practice work. Students such as Nick, who refuse to go along and do what for them is busy work and end up with lowered grades, receive grades that do not reflect their achievement.

Finally, including in grades practice work and/or learning activities can harm students who consistently improve. Consider the high school mathematics class with three formative quizzes and one summative test over a three-week period. Jeremy receives scores of 30, 50, and 70 percent on the quizzes and 90 percent on the test. He has obviously mastered whatever was taught over that unit. But if the quizzes count for one-third of the grade and the test for two-thirds (this is common) he would receive a grade of 77 percent, which in most high schools would be a C or worse.

The fix for all these broken grades is to not include scores from learning activities, including practice homework, in grades. One of the best ways to ensure this happens and to make the process clear to students is to develop assessment plans and (age appropriately) make them known to students.

An assessment plan should start with the desired results—the learning goals derived from the standards. The summative assessments that are going to be used to determine whether the student "knows and can do," (i.e., the only assessments that will be used to determine grades) follow. Next are the diagnostic assessment(s) that are going to help determine the what and the how for teaching and learning. Finally come the formative assessments that are going to help students achieve the learning goals and through which the teacher will adjust teaching and learning activities, such as the homework and quizzes that help students to be successful on tests, the practices that lead to performances, and the series of drafts that help students to produce high-quality products.

Figure 5.2 shows an example of the formative and summative assessment part of such a plan.

Note that in this plan there is a clear link between the formative and summative assessments—one or more practices of the role play with descriptive feedback will help students to perform high-quality role plays, one or more quizzes followed by analysis of strengths and weaknesses and appropriate reteaching will help students to be successful on the test(s), and the draft and near final versions of the product with descriptive feedback will lead to high-quality brochures. When a plan such as this is in place and students—and parents—are familiar with it, it is obvious to all that the focus is on the learning, not simply on the accumulation of points.

Quality school and district policy documents distinguish between formative and summative assessment and state clearly the uses of each, as in this from Manitoba:

Figure 5.2 Sample Assessment Plan

Formative Assessment for Unit 1

Task	Method(s)	Strategy(ies)	Scoring Tool	Assessor
ROLE PLAY Practice(s)	Performance Ass't	Performance	Rubric	Self/peer
QUIZZES	Paper and Pencil	Selected Response	Marking Scheme	Teacher
BROCHURE Draft	Performance Ass't	Product	Rubric	Peer
BROCHURE Near Final	Performance Ass't	Product	Rubric	Self/peer

Summative Assessment for Unit 1

Task	Method(s)	Strategy(ies)	Scoring Tool	Assessor
ROLE PLAY	Performance Ass't	Performance	Rubric	Teacher
TEST(S)	Paper and Pencil	Selected & Constructed Response	Marking Scheme	Teacher
BROCHURE	Performance Ass't	Product	Rubric	Teacher

Note: This assessment plan is for two standards taught in Unit 1 in a social studies course. The standards are not indicated in this plan.

The thrust of formative assessment is toward improving learning and instruction. Therefore, the information should not be used for assigning [grades] as the assessment often occurs before students have had full opportunities to learn content or develop skills. (Manitoba Education and Training, 1997, p. 9)

As a final idea in this Fix, I would like to note that this statement in the Manitoba policy and that made in the first paragraph of this Fix ("include only evidence from summative assessments intended to document learning") state the principle very strongly and clearly. However, once teachers have become clear about the appropriate uses for formative and summative assessment, and abandoned the practice of including everything in grades, especially homework, it is acceptable to *consider* formative assessment evidence when determining grades. This, of course, also requires that teachers are determining, not simply calculating, grades (see Fix 11). I acknowledge that I overstate when I say summative *"only"* but given traditional grading practices it seems to me that we have to establish this "strong" position; when teachers have developed a deeper understanding of grading issues, they can take a more holistic view of the evidence of achievement that each student has produced.*

Student Involvement

This is the most critical area for student involvement because students have often been "trained" in classrooms where no distinction was made between practice and performance and where there was little feedback or opportunities to make adjustments in learning (or teaching) based on formative assessment. Students who are actively involved in every aspect of assessment are more able to themselves distinguish between practice and performance. This can be achieved by encouraging self-monitoring and self-adjustment through assessment for learning and by avoiding rushing to judgment (summative assessment) for as long as possible. Stiggins and Chappuis (2005) describe strategies that teachers can use to involve students, including the following:

1. Engage students in reviewing strong and weak samples in order to determine attributes of a good performance or product. . . .
3. Students practice using criteria to evaluate anonymous strong and weak work.
4. Students work in pairs to revise an anonymous weak work sample they have just evaluated. (2005, p. 15)

Teachers can also help students to be reflective learners by providing them with opportunities to think about their performance on summative assessments. Stiggins and Chappuis suggest one way to do this:

9. Teacher arranges items on a test according to specific learning targets, and prepares a "test analysis" chart for student, with

---

*Anne Davies (personal communication, 2007) generously shared her knowledge and insights for this paragraph.

three boxes: "My strengths," "Quick review," and "Further study." After handing back the corrected test, students identify learning targets they have mastered and write them in the "My strengths" box. Next, students categorize their wrong answers as either "simple mistake" or "further study." Then, students list the simple mistakes in the "Quick review" box. Last, students write the rest of the learning targets represented by wrong answers in the "Further study" box. (2005, p. 15)

Summary

Grades are broken when they are merely about accumulating points. To make it obvious that they are about learning, the fix is to distinguish between formative and summative assessment and to include only results from the latter directly in grades.

> *The test of a successful education is not the amount of knowledge that a pupil takes away from school, but his appetite to know and his capacity to learn. If the school sends out children with the desire for knowledge and some idea about how to acquire it, it will have done its work. Too many leave school with the appetite killed and the mind loaded with undigested lumps of information. (Sir Richard Livingstone, President of Corpus Christi College, Oxford, 1941, quoted in Wiliam, 2003, n.p.)*

Teacher Vignette

Tom Schimmer, formerly Vice Principal, Princess Margaret Secondary School, BC

Our emphasis as administrators was on clearly identifying *practice*. As the year moved along, we began to see students with very low grades (e.g., 5%); grades that seemed, from our vantage point, quite difficult to achieve within a learning-focused school. As we discussed with our teachers the concern that students with very low grades tend to quit more often than improve, two issues came to light. The first was that many of the students hadn't completed their homework and, therefore, had received zeros in the gradebook. The zero lowers their grade, but when you have a significant number of zeros—more than 10 in the case of one teacher—the grade is obliterated to the point of no return. The other issue, relative to Fix 13, was students who had completed their homework but had received low scores. In discussions it was soon discovered that in some courses there was an overemphasis on *practice* that counted as part of grades and that the students in those classrooms never had the chance to practice new skills without the potential for penalty.

We focused on the need for practice and that students, when making a first attempt at practicing new learning, should be permitted to practice and take academic risks without having it cost them in the gradebook. We also emphasized that if *everything counts*, then the students' focus would be on compliance (meeting the deadline) through any means possible, including cheating. If task completion was our primary focus, then students will do whatever it takes to get it done. If learning is the priority and practice doesn't count, we emphasized, then the incentive to cheat is nullified. While in most cases homework is a small percentage of the final grade, it can have a significant impact. One gradebook we looked at contained 54 task entries in one term, the majority of which were homework entries. Students do whatever they can to *get work done*, at the expense of learning, when they know it is going to cost them.

The *fear* with implementing risk-free practice, of course, was, "If I don't grade it, they won't do it." Again, this fear was unfounded. Students saw the implementation of *practice* as more fair and reasonable. If everything counts, students will remain in their academic safe zone—only doing what they have done before and being satisfied with their level of achievement. When practice is not counted in grades students completed the work more often, took more chances, and pushed themselves to learn. Rather than giving scores and grades, we began to support teachers in the use of *descriptive feedback* with practice. This was the epitome of working backward; the emphasis on practice from a grading perspective led to our introduction and emphasis on descriptive feedback from a formative assessment perspective.

Policy Examples

Moanalua High School, Honolulu, HI

Purpose of Grading

The purpose of grading is to communicate student achievement of current Hawaii Content and Performance Standards (HCPS) to interested stakeholders (students, parents, colleges and other institutions).

Purpose of Schoolwide Grading Policy

The schoolwide grading policy implemented across all grade levels and disciplines shall:

- Provide teachers with guidelines to ensure common understandings of required practices and procedures to assess and evaluate student achievement fairly.

- Consistently and clearly communicate student achievement to all stakeholders.

Foundations of Standard-Based Grading

- Evidence of both formative and summative assessments shall be collected and recorded.

- Formative assessments shall be used to promote success in summative assessments.

- Formative assessments shall be evaluated with descriptive feedback.

- The purpose of formative assessments is to give reflective, thoughtful, meaningful feedback to the student and the teacher.

- Feedback of formative assessments directly helps students achieve learning goals and is a building block for summative assessments.

- Multiple opportunities shall be offered to students to provide evidence of learning.

Guiding Principles

Formative Assessments

Characteristics

Formative assessments:

- are student assignments that will help learners acquire skills to achieve standards.
- shall provide evidence of student progress.
- shall encourage risk-taking.
- shall prepare students for summative assessments.

Teacher Expectations and Responsibilities

Teachers shall:

- provide frequent, meaningful opportunities to practice skills and gauge/track progress.
- provide clearly defined processes and expectations to prepare students for summative assessments.
- provide accurate, specific, and timely descriptive feedback so that students can prepare for summative assessments.
- consider and utilize student feedback to improve the learning process.

Student Expectations and Responsibilities

Students shall:

- provide evidence in a timely manner within a grading period.
- use feedback to assess current progress to make improvements.
- provide feedback to teachers to improve assignments and methods.
- actively participate in the process.

Summative Assessments

Characteristics

Summative assessments:

- are final products and/or performances to evaluate student achievement of standards within a grading period.

Teacher Expectations and Responsibilities

Teachers shall:

- provide summative assessments that are based on previous teaching/learning and formative assessments.

- provide multiple/varied opportunities to demonstrate achievement within a grading period.
- provide clear criteria and expectations about how to achieve learning goals.
- provide clear and accurate feedback.
- consider and utilize student feedback to improve process.

Student Expectations and Responsibilities
Students shall:

- provide evidence in a timely manner within a grading period.
- use feedback to assess current progress to make improvements.
- provide feedback to teachers to improve assignments and methods.
- actively participate in the process.

Fix 14

Don't summarize evidence accumulated over time when learning is developmental and will grow with time and repeated opportunities; in those instances, emphasize more recent achievement.

The key question is, "What information provides the most accurate depiction of students' learning at this time?" In nearly all cases, the answer is "the most current information." If students demonstrate that past assessment information no longer accurately reflects their learning, that information must be dropped and replaced by the new information. Continuing to rely on past assessment data miscommunicates students' learning.

—Guskey, 1996a, p. 21

*G*rades are broken when learning is developmental (likely to improve over time with practice and repeated opportunities) and the final grade does not recognize the student's final level of proficiency. The fix for this type of broken grade is that for any developmental learning we must emphasize the more recent evidence and allow new evidence to replace, not simply be added to, old evidence.

Guskey says, "Educators generally recognize learning as a progressive and incremental process. Most also agree that students should have multiple opportunities to demonstrate their learning. But is it fair to consider all these learning trials in determining

120

students' grades? *If at any time in the instructional process students demonstrate that they have learned the concepts well and mastered the intended learning goals, doesn't that make all previous information on their learning of those concepts inaccurate and invalid?* Why then should such information be 'averaged in' when determining students' grades?" (Guskey, 2002, pp. 777–778, emphasis added).

Two very important issues emerge within this quotation as we think about grading developmental learning. First, by emphasizing the more recent information we acknowledge learning as a process and we can give students the message, "It is never over until it is really over!" One of the most unfortunate effects of simply adding up all the scores and calculating the mean is that many students will never be able to overcome the impact of early failures/very low scores. This is a terrible situation for both students and teacher because students who have no hope of success give up—and, as noted previously, frequently become discipline problems. If, however, our message to students is that we will acknowledge their learning whenever it occurs, then they have no reason to give up. In fact, this approach is a powerful motivator for students achieving at any level, because every student will know that improved achievement will get full recognition. Reeves (2000, p. 11) points out that the effective schools research shows that "one of the most consistent practices of successful teachers is the provision of multiple opportunities to learn. . . . The consequence for a student who fails to meet a standard is not a low grade but rather the opportunity, indeed the requirement—to resubmit his or her work."

The second issue Guskey's quotation raises concerns averaging. He indicates that with developmental learning, more recent information should not be simply averaged with outdated evidence when determining grades. Only the more recent data should be used. Fix 11 is relevant to this context. In it I propose that we see grading as an exercise in professional judgment, not just as a numerical, mechanical activity. The practical implication of this is that a common practice in high schools and middle schools must be abandoned—that of determining final grades by adding the grade for each grading period and dividing by the number of grading periods. Attempts have been made to devise a "power formula" or weighting to be applied when calculating grades that would emphasize more recent achievement while still allowing teachers to calculate grades, but none of these is as good as teacher judgment.

By emphasizing more recent evidence we acknowledge the impact of good teaching on student success. Consider the learning achievement curves of the four students in the graph shown in Figure 5.3.

Bob is basically the student who doesn't need a teacher, Gwen is a fairly typical successful student, while Roger and Pam need a lot of help. If all four of these students get the same grade, it will acknowledge their equally high achievement at the end. If Roger and Pam get lower grades, as they might traditionally, their achievement is misrepresented, which is academically unjustifiable.

If teachers really help students to meet standards and students then do so, this achievement needs to be recognized when grades are determined. For example, as part of the "effort-based intelligence" model within their "Framework for Improving Teaching and Learning," the Montgomery County (Maryland) Public Schools applies the criterion, "Staff shows tenacity to get students to meet standards"; the evidence that this tenacity bears fruit is then indicated by "a variety of student work that matches desired outcomes" (Montgomery County Public Schools, n.d., n.p.). For such a model to be truly effective, teachers will then assign students grades that accurately reflect their final achievement levels.

Summary

When learning is developmental and results from a process that unfolds over time so that student achievement increases with practice, the more recent evidence should "count" for the student's grade; old, outmoded evidence should be discarded. Grades are

Figure 5.3   Levels of Achievement over Time

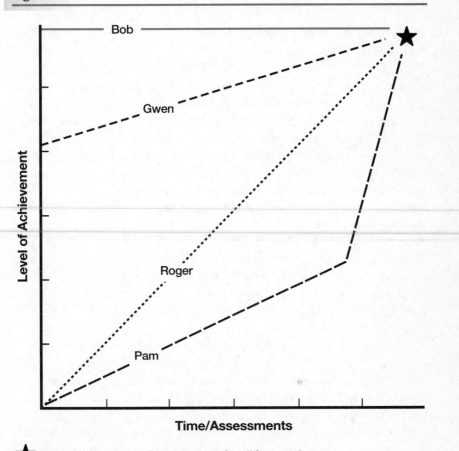

★ More Recent Level of Achievement for all four students
(represents several [2 or 3] pieces of evidence)

broken when this is not done. The fix is to emphasize more recent achievement, with more recent evidence replacing previous evidence.

What matters is not what you have at the starting point, but whether and how well you finish. (Gardner, 2002, n.p.)

Teacher Vignette

Melanie White, Bell High School, Ottawa-Carleton District School Board, ON

For the past five years, I have had a policy in my classroom that students can rewrite or redo any assessed and evaluated assignment so they can demonstrate learning and improvement. The expectation for any rewrite is that they must substantially change the content to improve the quality and that the changes must involve more than superficial changes such as grammar and mechanics. I ask students to attach the original assignment when they submit the rewrite. By having the two assignments to compare, I can better assess the learning of the student and give them more feedback for improvement; additionally I can show them how they demonstrated their learning. Students frequently comment that they feel more secure in getting concrete feedback, in having opportunities, and that they feel like they can make mistakes and learn from them while working toward a goal that they establish for themselves. I often compare this for my students to the concept of video games where failure is an expected part of learning to progress in the game and that the only way to improve in a given game is through persistence on a particular task. If they persist at writing, they will improve.

In my English classes, experience has shown me that about one third of the students take advantage of rewrites and the marking of the rewritten assignment is quicker for me than marking the assignment for the first time. I have not found that students underperform on the original submission of assignments. I can only speculate as to the reasons, but I think they do not want to have to rewrite assignments where possible, so they still put forth effort with each assessment or evaluation. Those students who are motivated to improve their mark take the feedback, are able to apply this to the rewrite, and feel less anxiety knowing that they have some control over their mark in a given course. My experience has taught me that they often tell me they will rewrite assignments, and have intentions to do so, but ultimately they do not follow through and this is why I think only about one-third of students ever take advantage of rewrites.

Policy Example

St. Michaels University School, Victoria, BC

3. Determination of Grades

Weighting performance over time: Teachers are to ensure that a student's grade accurately reflects his/her best mastery of particular outcomes. Where a student has demonstrated significant improvement in terms of mastery of particular outcomes through the year, the *more recent evidence* should be emphasized in the determination of the grade. *This eliminates the need to "average" marks in any calculation.*

Fix 15

Don't leave students out of the grading process. Involve students; they can—and should—play key roles in assessment and grading that promote achievement.

We must constantly remind ourselves that the ultimate purpose of evaluation is to enable students to evaluate themselves. Educators may have been practicing this skill to the exclusion of learners; we need to shift part of that responsibility to students. Fostering students' ability to direct and redirect themselves must be a major goal . . . or what is education for?

—Costa, 1991, p. 313

Grades—and assessment—are broken if teachers simply "run the show." Students must be involved in all stages of the assessment process and should understand (age appropriately) from the outset how grades will be determined. Students can learn how to monitor their own progress, and how to communicate that progress to others. In so doing, they understand more deeply their own strengths and areas needing improvement, and can use that understanding to guide specific, meaningful goal-setting about what they can learn/do next. Ideas about student involvement have appeared in several of this book's Fixes. Fix 15 is a summary and restatement of the key ideas.

Grades should communicate achievement status, and both assessment and grading need to help students achieve at higher levels and develop positive attitudes about learning. These things are more likely to happen when students are involved as active participants in ongoing assessment and grading, so that they see the entire process as something that is done with them, not to them. Teachers also benefit when they share with students from the beginning how they will determine grades. It is also important that students (and parents) receive short, clear written statements about grading policy/procedures. Figure 5.4 shows an example of such a policy.

We must be mindful of the fact that students are users of the information that comes from assessments, so the purpose of each assessment must be clear to them. We must also be sure that students understand the targets; there are many strategies that can be used to help them with this* but one of the most powerful is to involve them in developing the rubrics we use to provide feedback and/or scores. Probably the most important aspect of student involvement is having them track their progress and achievement and then communicate about their learning with other students, teachers, and significant adults in their life. One way to do this is to use assessment plans, such as the one shown in Figure 5.2. It is the teacher's responsibility to evaluate the summative assessments, but students should be involved in peer and self-assessment of formative assessments. This allows them to practice the skills of self-assessment and to deepen their understanding of the conditions of quality. As Chappuis (2009) states, "Providing students with opportunities for a combination of peer feedback and self-assessment causes them to achieve at significantly higher levels, without more instruction. These two practices increase their sense of ownership of the responsibility to learn" (p. 96).

*See, for example, the "Seven Strategies of Assessment *for* Learning" in Stiggins et al., 2004, pp. 42–46; and Chappuis, 2009.

Figure 5.4   Mrs. Greier's Grading Practices

Grading: Grades will be based on mastery of the Sunshine State Standards.

Formative Assessment

This type of assessment is for practice only. It will not be averaged for the report card grade.

Examples include but are not limited to the following:

- Daily Work—Center work, group assignments, math practice, etc.
- Homework—Every Monday your child will write their homework assignments for that week in their homework folder. Please sign the homework sheet that is in his/her folder and have your child bring it back to school on Tuesday. Your child will have math homework every night and is due the next morning. On Thursday morning, all other homework assignments will be collected. These assignments must be completed in order to receive privileges such as Fun Friday and other events.

You will be contacted via phone or letter if your child is not completing assignments.

Today's Homework Makes
Tomorrow's Home Work

Summative Assessment

This type of assessment will "sum" or measure what your child has learned. A grade will be assigned to the work and goes in the gradebook following several opportunities for the student to practice the skill.

Examples include but are not limited to the following:

- Pencil and paper test
- Performance task—The student will be asked to perform a skill such as properly measuring liquids.
- Presentation—Student presents material he or she has learned in the form of book talks, reports, etc.
- Rubric—Rubrics are used on many summative assessments. The student is assessed on a number scale according to their achievement.

Grading Scale

90–100 A   80–89 B   70–79 C   60–69 D   0–59 F

Figure 5.4 Mrs. Greier's Grading Practices (continued)

Expectations
Be respectful and responsible
Encourage others
Always do your best
Care and cooperate
Have the courage to try

I have read and understand this grading policy.

Student_____   Parent_____

When students have become self-assessors who are reflective learners they then communicate with parents or significant adults about their strengths, areas for improvement, and next steps in their learning. This means that schools/districts need to set up their communication system to include student-involved or student-led conferences from kindergarten through high school. This type of conference has been found to have a significant impact on students taking responsibility for their own learning and to result in better parent attendance.

Summary

Grades are broken when students do not understand how their grades have been determined, and when they have been excluded from assessment, record keeping, and communication. The fix is to ensure that students understand how grades have been determined and to involve them as much as possible in all phases of learning and assessment.

As students become more involved in the assessment process, teachers find themselves working differently. . . . Many teachers are spending less time marking at the end of learning and more time helping students during the learning. (Davies, 2000, p. 9)

Teacher Vignette

Danielle Caldwell, Richmond School District, BC

When using literature circles with my grade 8s and my grade 11s, I tell them the learning outcomes and why we are doing literature circles. I find the students are far better engaged and they prefer the activity better when they know their targets. In this case I tell them not only the learning outcomes, but also the summative assessment. We also identify key essential questions, which guide them throughout the unit.

One of our learning outcomes is to interact and collaborate in small groups to develop their oral language skills. Before we begin I show them a sample rubric. After we have talked about what a good discussion looks and sounds like and they have watched me model one with colleagues, each group is then given a blank rubric where they set the standards for their group discussions, based on the members of their group. This is an example of how to actively engage students in establishing their own valid and meaningful assessment criteria.

I have found that the key to success with my students is that they understand the learning outcomes, they have set the guidelines that indicate their success, and at the end of each literature circle they assess how they performed. Two of the circles are formative and the third is summative.

Not only do they peer assess on the oral, they also do so with their journal entries in a format that has been dubbed by my 8s as "We're triple peeing again" (Praise, Polish, Ponder). I am impressed with their growth. They have moved from what began as Praise: "good job"; Polish: Nothing; Ponder: What is dung? to Praise: "Your connection to the homeless is a good one when you compare Alyce living in the Dung, before she was found by the midwife"; Polish: Maybe try saying why Alyce is like the homeless today with more reasons why she is the same; Ponder: Why do we still have so many homeless people? Life has changed but there still are homeless people? (taken from a student's journal, Humanities 8). My students have grown, they peer assess, and they have taken on the ownership of seeing the value of what makes a good journal entry based on criteria which we earlier established as a class. They are the ones actively engaged in the learning, working and supporting each other.

In creating the learning environment this way, my students are able to choose which pieces they submit when it is time for the summative assessment. They have had many opportunities to practice. They are familiar with the terminology and comfortable with the process. Even for oral presentations, we will do a formative run through and automatically the students will 3P the presenters. They are accurate and sincere. I sit back in awe and ask myself—do they need me and how did this happen? They are shaping their learning. But is this not what we want?

Policy Example

Halifax Regional School Board Assessment, Evaluation and Communication of Student Learning Policy and Procedures (Revised September 24, 2008)

Policy

2.1 While students are the most important users of all assessment information, the Halifax Regional School Board recognizes that classroom assessment has a variety of audiences. For each of these audiences, classroom assessment will serve the following primary purposes:

2.1.1 Students: To enhance the learning, motivation, and confidence of students, helping them develop skills and strategies as self-assessors who are responsible for their own learning;

Procedures

Classroom Assessment

Teachers are responsible for:

1.2.6 Evaluating student learning by: . . .

    1.2.6.2 Communicating criteria for evaluation with students before the process of learning, assessing, evaluating, and reporting occurs. The criteria and guidelines can be teacher generated, student generated, or developed collaboratively and, where possible, will be accompanied by examples of quality performance or product for each level of proficiency;

1.2.7 Involving students in the assessment and evaluation process by:

    1.2.7.1 Discussing achievement targets and classroom assessment practices with students, in an age-appropriate manner, at the beginning of instruction and continuing this conversation on an ongoing basis;

    1.2.7.2 Ensuring that students have a range of opportunities and ways to demonstrate their knowledge, skills, and attitudes pertaining to expected learning outcomes by using multiple assessment strategies;

        1.2.7.2.3 Helping students to understand and communicate the expected learning outcomes for which they are responsible, as well as the criteria that will be used to evaluate their work. Whenever possible students should be involved in creating the criteria;

        1.2.7.2.4 Giving students a variety of samples of student work (exemplars) to help them understand what quality looks like and what is required to achieve the expected learning outcomes;

        1.2.7.2.5 Providing timely, descriptive feedback of what each student knows and is able to do in relation to the expected learning outcomes, and how the student can improve in relation to those outcomes;

> 1.2.7.2.6 Providing opportunities for students to give descriptive feedback to each other.

Students are responsible for:

1.4.1 Accepting responsibility and ownership for their own learning through active involvement in the assessment and evaluation process in order to discover how they learn best and to understand exactly where they are in relation to the defined curriculum outcomes.

Chapter 6

Summary

The best thing you can do is make sure your grades convey meaningful, accurate information about student achievement. If grades give sound information to students, then their perceptions (and) conclusions about themselves as learners, and decisions about future activity will be the best they can be.

—Brookhart, 2004, p. 34

Grades are summary symbols that should communicate only about student achievement at a point in time. To be effective, they must be consistent, accurate, and meaningful, and should support learning. Unfortunately, because grading has often been an unexamined and private practice, grades have frequently not met these standards and as a result are very often broken. In this book I have described 15 Fixes for broken grades—fixes for ingredients that distort achievement, low-quality or poorly organized evidence, inappropriate grade calculation, and lack of support for learning.

Linking the Fixes to these standards, for consistency Fix 8 needs to be in place. For accuracy, Fixes 1 to 6 and 9 to 12 need to be used. For grades to be meaningful, Fix 7 needs to be applied. And to support learning, Fixes 13, 14, and 15 need to be implemented.

This is a long list, and implementing the Fixes is not easy. Achievement in standards-based systems equals mastering those standards. Required content and performance standards must be clear and must be the focus of curriculum, instruction, assessment, grading, and reporting. Assessment must be accurate and the *process* of learning emphasized by involving students in assessment, record keeping, and communication.

Practically, any one (or more) of the Fixes can be used as a starting point. But effective grading in standards-based systems really flows from Fix 7 because as soon as one is truly standards-based in assessment and grading the other Fixes become logical extensions. When grading is only about achievement of standards it quickly becomes obvious that it is inappropriate to include factors other than achievement (1–6), that it is necessary to have quality evidence (8–10) that accurately summarizes student achievement (11, 12), and that the emphasis needs to be on the learning process itself (13–15).

I believe that there are two "givens" that cannot be questioned in all schools:

1. All assessments must be of high quality.
2. Students must be involved in the assessment process.

There are also six "musts" that can be questioned with regard to details and implementation but not the basic principles involved:

1. Standards-based curriculum, instruction, assessment, grading, and reporting with no single-subject grades except for grades 11 and 12

2. Performance standards with clear descriptions of a limited number of levels with no use of percentages

3. Achievement separated from behaviors with no mark penalties for late work, academic dishonesty, or attendance

4. Summative assessments providing (almost) all the evidence for determining grades with no mark; comment-only formative assessment

5. More recent evidence emphasized in the determination of grades when learning is cumulative and developmental

6. Careful and limited number crunching with no zeros and use of professional judgment and the use of median and mode in addition to or in place of the mean

Teachers, schools, and districts need to examine their grading procedures and policies to see if they "fit" with what is expected in standards-based systems. Changes in grading practices will occur when teachers engage in professional dialogue about grading and agree on guidelines that avoid the inappropriate use and interpretation of grades. Fixes such as those described here can be the basis for such guidelines and those guidelines can then be incorporated into school board and school grading policies.

It is my intent and hope in writing this book that teachers will become reflective practitioners in the area of grading and that the 15 Fixes will form the basis for grades that are consistent, accurate, and meaningful, and that support learning.

Neither computerized calculations nor rigorously applied grading systems are enough to save schools from some of the most common and egregious errors in grading. Amazingly, teachers

*regularly use and leaders tolerate grading systems that may
appear to be accurate but are devoid of the most basic elements
of mathematical reasoning and are neither fair nor effective.
(Reeves, 2006, p. 119)*

A Repair Kit for Grading

15 Fixes for Broken Grades

DISCUSSION GUIDE

Introduction

A Repair Kit for Grading describes 15 ways to make grades and marks more consistent, accurate, meaningful, and supportive of learning. This guide is intended to help process some of the ideas presented in the book and can be used individually or in conjunction with learning team–based study of the book.

The book represents one of three related resources from Pearson Assessment Training Institute on the topic of grading to support learning. The other two are as follows:

- The DVD *Grading and Reporting in Standards-Based Schools* features Ken O'Connor and Rick Stiggins of Pearson ATI giving an interactive workshop experience about grading/marking interspersed with opportunities to discuss the information presented.

- The third source for information on grading is Pearson ATI's *Classroom Assessment* for *Student Learning: Doing It Right-Using It Well (CASL)* (Stiggins et al., 2004). Chapter 10 examines sound grading practices, and additional information in other chapters bears on the topics in this book.

Discussion Questions Applicable to All of the Fixes

Following are discussion questions/activities specific to each of the Fixes. However, learning teams can also apply the same template to every Fix as a consistent discussion, as in the following examples:

- After reading this Fix, what did you find that was positive, what was/is a minus in your view, and what did you find that was new or interesting? Please elaborate or explain your answer.

- After reading the Fix, how does this compare to the current grading practice in your classroom/school/district? Do you think any changes should be made to current practice given your understanding of the Fix?

Discussion Questions and Activities

Activity 1.1 Self-Assessing Your Grading Practices

Purpose: To think about and record your current grading practices for later comparison purposes

Activities: Appendix A contains the ATI rubric for evaluating grading practices. Mark or highlight the words and phrases in the rubric that reflect your current practice, and then put this aside for future use. Appendix B presents a survey about current grading practices and beliefs. Take the survey, and also put it aside for later use.

Activity 1.2 Your Questions about Grading

Purpose: To identify questions and issues you have at this time related to sound grading practice

Activity: Individually or as a group write down the questions you have about any aspect of grading. As with the activity above, we'll ask you to revisit this list later at the end of study.

Chapter 2: Fixes for Practices That Distort Achievement

Activity 2.1 Factors to Include In Grades

Fixes 1–6: These six fixes urge readers to not include any of the following in grades—student behaviors, reduced marks on work submitted late, points for extra credit, marks for bonus questions on tests or exams, reduced marks for cheating, attendance, or group scores.

Purpose: To examine the reasons that student behaviors (Fix 1), reduced marks on work submitted late (Fix 2), points for extra credit and marks for bonus questions on tests or exams (Fix 3), academic dishonesty (Fix 4), attendance (Fix 5), and/or group scores (Fix 6) should not be included in grades

Activity: Choose one or more of the factors listed in Fixes 1–6. Then, generate a list of reasons FOR including the chosen factor in grades, and arguments AGAINST doing so. Arguments for and against each factor can be found under Fixes 1–6 in *A Repair Kit for Grading*; additional arguments for some of the factors follow.

After completing both sections discuss what conclusions you draw about including factors besides achievement into grades/marks. Has your thinking changed on any of these factors over time? As a result of this exercise? Not at all? Why?

Fix 1: Effort

Arguments FOR including effort in grades	**Arguments AGAINST including effort in grades**
■ Effort is a valued outcome for students and should be rewarded.	■ Including effort muddies the degree to which students have attained mastery of learning targets.
■ Including effort provides some reward to low achievers.	■ Effort is difficult to define and assess well.
■ Awarding effort should motivate students to complete work.	■ Most effort is expended outside the classroom.
■ Awarding effort can underpin risk taking (innovative effort that falls short), a valued outcome for students.	■ Students can manipulate the teacher's perception of effort.
	■ Different teachers use different weights when including effort in grades.
	■ In some cases, the teacher controls who participates.
	■ Personality traits or cultural differences can affect the appearance of effort.
■ While aptitude is not under students' control, effort is.	■ Life demands achievement—not just trying hard.
■ Current research suggests that students learn better if success or failure is attributed to effort rather than ability.	■ What do we value—achieving or achieving and making it look hard? What if it was easy?
	■ Praise for effort only works if a success at learning is attributed to effort; effort praised in and of itself can lead to less motivation if a student fails yet is praised for effort.

Fix 2: Reducing Marks for Work Submitted Late

Arguments FOR reducing marks for work submitted late	**Arguments AGAINST reducing marks for work submitted late**
■ It rewards students who turn their work in on time so that grading time is minimized and the pace of learning is maintained.	■ It muddies the degree to which students have mastered the desired learning targets.
■ Promptness is valued in real life.	■ It can mask the reasons for the late work, decreasing the chances that the school can help.
■ It is most fair to students to give everyone the same amount of time.	■ Such penalties don't work for many chronically late students.
■ Students who do work on time learn more.	■ If the goal is to change behavior rather than to punish noncompliance, there may be more effective procedures.
	■ In daily life many deadlines are regularly renegotiated.

Fix 3: Points for Extra Credit

Arguments FOR including points for extra credit in grades when they reflect something other than the expected learning	Arguments AGAINST including points for extra credit in grades when they reflect something other than the expected learning
■ It provides a means of giving students the grade one feels is appropriate ■ It is seen to be motivating and fun so that students want to do the work ■ Doing extra credit is an indicator of effort.	■ It muddies the degree to which a student has attained mastery of content. ■ It can be difficult to determine how much extra credit is logical. ■ Different teachers can have different amounts of extra credit. ■ It may send an unwanted message to students about what the learning targets are.

Fix 3: Points for Bonus Questions

Arguments FOR including points for bonus questions in grades	Arguments AGAINST including points for bonus questions in grades
■ It provides a way for students to get more points and get better grades. ■ It is seen to be motivating to give students more points for being willing to answer more questions. ■ Doing bonus questions is an indicator of effort.	■ It muddies the degree to which a student has attained mastery of content. ■ It can be difficult to determine how many bonus questions are appropriate. ■ Different teachers can have different amounts of bonus questions. ■ Bonus questions are almost always conceptual or involve higher-order thinking skills and should be part of the test for all students.

Activity 2.2 What's in a "B"?

Fixes 1, 2, 3, 5, 8, 13, and 14: Don't include any of the following in grades—student behaviors, reduced marks on work submitted late, points for extra credit, attendance, ability, homework, and early work.

Purpose: To examine the problems associated with including factors besides achievement in grades

Activity: Read the following scenario and discuss the subsequent questions.

A group of teachers, other educators, and parents were attending a grading workshop at a regional conference. A parent asked if the educators in the room could tell her what's in a B and how it is different from an A or C. Participants were asked to record their answers to two questions:

1. What should a grade tell us about students?
2. What factors are actually used to determine student grades in your setting?

The answers were compiled into two charts:

What Should Grades Tell Us About Students?	What Factors Are Actually Included in Grades?
■ What things they know and can do ■ Whether they have improved during the marking period ■ What their strengths are and the things they need to work on ■ Whether they can solve real-world problems ■ What level their work is at ■ Whether they are ready to move on ■ How they help one another ■ Whether they've reached a standard ■ How well they can apply what they know	■ Achievement ■ Attendance and tardiness ■ Behavior/attitude ■ End of marking period test scores ■ Homework ■ Family status ■ Ability ■ Promptness in getting work in ■ Extra credit bonus points

How closely does the list on the left reflect what you think grades should tell us about students?

Now look at the list on the right. Would these factors, when included in grades, help provide the information needed for the decisions on the left? What would need to be done differently? What things on either list are problematic for you or do you have trouble supporting? Why?

Activity 2.3 Encouraging Promptness

Fix 2: Don't reduce marks on work submitted late.

Purpose: To consider replacement strategies for encouraging students to get work in on time

Discuss: For Fix 2, Ken suggests that marking/grading penalties for late work misrepresent student achievement, harm student motivation, and are generally ineffective in changing behavior. Discuss the pros and cons of the suggested alternative strategies (following), then brainstorm other solutions you have seen or used. Which of these might you be willing to try in your own classroom?

Suggestions:

- Direct communication with parents
- Require structured study hall before, during, or after school
- Identify at the beginning of the school year students who are organizationally challenged and provide them structure in assignments
- Involve students in deciding timelines and consequences for lateness
- Negotiate extension of time as needed based on reasonable need

Activity 2.4 Academic Dishonesty

Fix 4: Don't punish academic dishonesty with reduced grades.

Purpose: To consider replacement strategies for punishing academic dishonesty with reduced grades

Discuss: For Fix 4, Ken suggests that there are two main issues surrounding cheating: how to prevent it, and what to do about it when it happens. He proposes several answers to each question, summarized here. Discuss these ideas in turn, and how/why they might or might not work for you.

How to Prevent Cheating	What to Do When Cheating Occurs
Articulate an academic honesty policy with clear behavioral consequences for breaches, such as providing evidence of level of achievement through redoing the current assignment or completing another exam or assignment; communicating the misconduct to all the student's teachers; complete the work on his/her own time; suspend extracurricular involvement; probation; suspension; expulsion.	Interview students privately to try and determine if the transgression was inadvertent or deliberate. If inadvertent, counsel the student and require the work to be redone. If deliberate, apply the sanctions in the district policy.
Make expectations clear to students and help them understand why academic integrity is so important.	
Make the meaning of plagiarism and cheating clear to students. For example, show an example of plagiarism.	
Use in-class assignments.	

Change exams each term.	
Proctor exams; spread students out during exams; use extended written response formats; check back packs, coats, and technology.	
Have students attach a signed statement to all summative assessments and assignments that they have not cheated or plagiarized.	

Activity 2.6 Borderline Grades

End of Chapter 2

Purpose: To consider replacement strategies for assigning borderline grades based on behavior, attendance, and so on

Discuss: What do you do if you have a borderline grade? Ken advises not to consider attendance, effort, participation, and so on when making a decision. Rather, he suggests the need to gather more evidence, and suggests several sources of additional information. What are the pros and cons of these suggestions? Add ideas and discuss what might work for you.

1. Give the students an oral test—three well-crafted questions asked and answered in ten minutes will provide much additional evidence.
2. Have an additional assignment or test at hand to use for tie-breaking.
3. Homework or other practice work, used with care, might provide extra evidence.
4. Engage students as partners in identifying appropriate evidence of learning.
5. Give more comprehensive assessments and assignments greater weight.

Chapter 3: Fixes for Low-Quality or Poorly Organized Evidence

Activity 3.1 Setting Up Record Books

Fix 7: Don't organize information in grading records by assessment methods

Purpose: To consider replacement strategies for setting up a record book by source of information rather than learning goal

Discuss: In Fix 7, Ken discusses various ways that record books can be set up to reflect learning goals for students rather than sources of information (quizzes, tests, etc.) He talks about both the need to decide the level of detail about goals to be kept (by standard, benchmark/grade-level expectation/objective, or specific targets) and keeping a separate page of information for each student.

Consider your own record-keeping system now. Does it reflect any aspect of this description? If not, how might you set up a learning record book by learning goal? What level of detail would it be necessary to include?

Chapter 4: Fixes for Inappropriate Grade Calculation

Activity 4.1 Teacher Judgment

Fix 11: Don't rely only on the mean; consider other measures of central tendency.

Purpose: To explore when teacher judgment might be included and may result in a summative grade that is different from that calculated by a measure of central tendency of scores

Discussion: The book presents the difference between *determining* grades and *calculating* grades. What happens when teachers use professional judgment to augment numerical calculations and a final judgment doesn't strictly match the numerical calculation? When might this happen? Why might a teacher choose that option? How might such a procedure be justified? Not justified?

Activity 4.2 Including Zeros

Fix 12: Don't include zeros in grade determination when evidence is missing or as punishment

Purpose: To consider replacement strategies for using zeros for missing or late work

Discuss: Ken provides several suggestions for handling missing information when determining grades. Discuss which of these alternatives would be a good fit in your classroom.

1. If the missing work is practice work, such as most homework, it shouldn't be included in a final grade anyway (Fix 13).
2. If the missing work is necessary in order to determine level of proficiency, use *incomplete* instead of a grade (Fix 12). Accompany this with specific requirements for completing the work, e.g., Saturday work sessions.
3. The use of zeros is problematic because they have such an impact

on averages. A transition strategy might be to assign 50 percent for missing work, making the range for an F (50–60%) roughly the same for other grades (e.g., A is 90–100%; Fix 12).

4. For the same reason as in solution 3, you might make the scale "equal interval" by using A = 4, B = 3, C = 2, D = 1, and F = 0 (Fix 12).
5. Again, for the same reason as in solution 3, you might use the median score instead of the mean (Fix 12).
6. Build overlapping assessments so that if a student misses any one of them there will be enough evidence from the others (Fix 12).
7. Require that students supply extra evidence of learning so that proficiency level can be accurately determined. Have a store of assignments or tests on hand and require that students complete them (Fix 2).

Activity 4.3 The Dilemma of the Zero

Fix 12: Don't include zeros in grade determination when evidence is missing or as punishment

Purpose: To discuss a solution to a real situation involving including zeros in grades

Activity: Read the following scenario:

Your daughter is enrolled in a 10th-grade biology course. The midterm report sent home from school says she is getting a D+ in biology, yet the only tests and assignments you have seen have had A and B+ on the top. Your daughter reports having done all the required work and is at a loss to explain the grade. You request a meeting with the teacher.

The teacher explains that the grade is based on actual performance so your daughter must not be learning the material. The teacher uses a computer grade book software program. He enters your daughter's name and the screen shows a list of entries leading to an average of 69 percent. The teacher points out that the cutoff scores he has placed in the computer transforms this percentage into a D+. So the report is correct.

Here is the information on the screen:

First unit test:	95%
Unit lab report	85%
Second test:	85%
Unit lab report	0%

You inquire about the "0%." If the report is missing, the computer is instructed to enter a zero into the record and average it into the computation of the grade. But, you point out, your child seems to be grasping the material fairly well and performing well on the required assessments. The teacher seems genuinely surprised at the reason for the low grade, agreeing that the rest of the record is very good. How is it, you ask, that the teacher concluded earlier that your child is not learning the material?

Upon further discussion, you find that she had specifically asked for permission to turn in the report late because she wanted to work further on the data analysis, and she was granted permission to do so. The teacher has no recollection of that conversation.

Discuss:

1. Are the teacher's practices in this case sound from a grading point of view? Why or why not?
2. If you were this teacher what might you have done to avoid this problem?

Chapter 5: Fixes to Support Learning

Activity 5.1 Using Formative Information Summatively

Fix 13: Don't use information from formative assessments and practice to determine grades; use only summative assessment.

Purpose: To examine when using formative data to inform a summative decision might be legitimate

Discuss: Ken writes, "Include, in all but specific, limited cases, only evidence from summative assessments. . . ." What might be some of the limited, specific cases in which evidence from formative work can be considered when determining a final grade?

Following are two other ideas. Does either of these sound reasonable? Why or why not?

1. A borderline grade might be resolved by considering the entire body of evidence for a student including formative work such as drafts and practices. In order for this to work, a teacher needs to have in mind what A, B, C, etc. understanding looks like, not just consider the total number of points earned.
2. Student learning targets that require complex and lengthy performances or creation of products can be tricky for strictly separating formative and summative assessments. Consider lab reports. Say a teacher assigns 10 labs over the course of a semester so that students can practice and get better over time. To strictly separate formative and summative assessments, after the 10th report, the students would be assigned some number of reports to create, the marks to count toward the final grade. But, this is unwieldy and time con-

suming. Why not just use performance on the final two or three lab reports as summative assessment?

End-of-Book Discussion Questions

Activity 6.1 Grading Policy

Purpose: To consider what features would be useful to include in a policy statement on grading

Discuss: Various school and district policies are presented throughout *A Repair Kit for Grading.* Many of these examples represent one or more of the Fixes described, with some of them listed here. With your group discuss which of these you would like to see or not see in *your* local grading policy statement.

- Grades and marks should reflect only achievement not effort, participation, attendance, lateness of work, extra credit not related to our learning goals, nor academic dishonesty (Fixes 1–5).

- Behavior is important and will be reported and acted on, but using a more effective procedure than reducing grades (Fixes 1–5).

- If there is not enough evidence of a student's level of proficiency because of missing summative information, the student will receive an *incomplete* (Fixes 2, 4, and 12). Zeros for missing work will not be averaged into grades. Students will have _____ amount of time to convert this incomplete to a grade by submitting additional evidence of proficiency. The student is responsible for discussing with the teacher the evidence that would be acceptable. And/or students are required to join a Saturday work session.

- Scores for group work will not be included in marks/grades (Fix 6).

- All summative grades will be based on clearly defined standards for performance, not performance compared to other students (Fixes 8 and 9).

- All grades will be based on accurate assessment information (Fix 10).

- Grades will be based on the most consistent pattern of performance, not just on the average score or rating. This means that sometimes the median or the mode provides the most accurate measure of performance (Fix 11). This also means that for proficiencies that develop over time, performance at the end is more important than performance at the beginning (Fix 14). Additionally, this means that grades may not be based on strictly numerical computations. There is a role for teacher judgment of proficiency (Fix 11).

- Performance on work intended for practice will only be considered in the final grade if it provides extra evidence of proficiency (Fix 13).

- Feedback to students on practice work will be descriptive rather than evaluative (Fix 13).

- Students and parents will know from the beginning of instruction which assessments are for practice and which will count toward the final grade (Fix 13).

- Other ideas can be found in various policy statements on pages 117–119.

Activity 6.2 Where Am I Now?

Purpose: To think about how your grading practices and/or understanding and opinions about grading practices have evolved since the beginning of study

Activity: Appendix A is the Pearson ATI rubric for grading practices. Appendix B is a survey about current grading practices and beliefs. Using these appendices, self-assess your grading practices now in the same manner as you did in Activity 1.1. Then analyze what has changed on each instrument. Why? What does that mean for your classroom practice? What will be different?

Activity 6.3 Questions About Grading

Purposes: To revisit your initial questions and determine which you can now answer

Activity: Look at your initial questions from Activity 1.2. How might you answer these questions now? What new questions have arisen? If you are working in a team, how do your new questions and responses to previous questions compare to others in your group?

Appendix A
Rubric for Evaluating Grading Practices

Criterion	Beginning	Developing	Fluent
1. Organizing the gradebook	The evidence of learning (e.g., a gradebook) is entirely organized by sources of information (e.g., tests, quizzes, homework, labs, etc.).	The evidence of learning (e.g., a gradebook) is organized by sources of information mixed with specific content standards.	The evidence of learning (e.g., a gradebook) is completely organized by student learning outcomes (e.g., content standards, benchmarks, grade level indicators, curriculum expectations, etc.).
2. Including factors in the grade	Overall summary grades are based on a mix of achievement and nonachievement factors (e.g., timeliness of work, attitude, effort, cheating). Non-achievement factors have a major impact on grades. Extra credit points are given for extra work completed; without connection to extra learning. Cheating, late work, and missing work result in a zero (or a radically lower score) in the gradebook. There is no opportunity to make up such work, except in a few cases. Borderline grade cases are handled by considering non-achievement factors.	Overall summary grades are based on a mix of achievement and nonachievement factors, but achievement counts a lot more. Some extra credit points are given for extra work completed; some extra credit work is used to provide extra evidence of student learning. Cheating, late work, and missing work result in a zero (or lower score) in the gradebook. But, there is an opportunity to make up work and replace the zero or raise the lower score. Borderline cases are handled by considering a combination of nonachievement factors and collecting additional evidence of student learning.	Overall summary grades are based on achievement only. Extra credit work is evaluated for quality and is only used to provide extra evidence of learning. Credit is not awarded merely for completion of work. Cheating, late work, and missing work is recorded as "incomplete" or "not enough information" rather than as zero. There is an opportunity to replace an "incomplete" with a score without penalty. Borderline grade cases are handled by collecting additional evidence of student achievement, not by counting nonachievement factors.
3. Considering assessment purpose	Everything each student does is given a score and every score goes into the final grade. There is no distinction between "scores" on practice work (formative assessment or many types of homework) and scores on work to demonstrate level of achievement (summative assessment).	Some distinctions are made between formative (practice such as homework) and summative assessment, but practice work still constitutes a significant part of the grade.	Student work is assessed frequently (formative assessment) and graded occasionally (summative assessment). "Scores" on formative assessments and other practice work (e.g., homework) are used descriptively to inform teachers and students of what has been learned and the next steps in learning. Grades are based only on summative assessments.

Rubric for Evaluating Grading Practices *(continued)*

Criterion	Beginning	Developing	Fluent
4. Considering most recent information	All assessment data is cumulative and used in calculating a final summative grade. No consideration is given to identifying or using the most current information.	More current evidence is given consideration at times, but does not entirely replace out-of-date evidence.	Most recent evidence completely replaces out-of-date evidence when it is reasonable to do so. For example, how well students write at the end of the grading period is more important than how well they write at the beginning, and later evidence of improved content understanding is more important than early evidence.
5. Summarizing information and determining final grade	The gradebook has a mixture of ABC, precentages, + ✓ –, and/or rubric scores, etc., with no explanation of how they are to be combined into a final summary grade. Rubric scores are converted to percentages when averaged with other scores; or, there is no provision for combining rubric and percentage scores. Final summary grades are based on a curve—a student's place in the rank order of student achievement. Final grades for special needs students are not based on learning targets as specified in the IEP. Final summary grades are based on caluclation of mean (average) only.	The gradebook may or may not have a mixture of symbols, but there is some attempt, even if incomplete, to explain how to combine them. Rubric scores are not directly converted to percentages; some type of decision rule is used, the final grade many times does not best depict level of student achievement. Final grades are criterion referenced, not norm referenced. They are based on preset standards such as A = 90–100% and B = 80–89%. But, there is no indication of the necessity to ensure shared meaning of symbols—i.e., there is no definition of each standard. There is an attempt to base final grades for special needs students on learning targets in the IEP, but the attempt is not always successful; or, it is not clear to all parties that modified learning targets are used to assign a grade. The teacher understands various measures of central tendency, but may not always choose the best one to accurately describe student achievement.	The gradebook may or may not have a mix of symbol types, but there is a sound explanation of how to combine them. Rubric scores are converted to a final grade using a decision rule that results in an accurate depiction of the level of student attainment of the learning targets. Final grades are criterion referenced, not norm referenced. They are based on preset standards with clear descriptions of what each symbol means. These descriptions go beyond A = 90–100% and B = 80–89%; they describe what A, B, etc. performance looks like. Final grades for special needs students are criterion referenced, and indicate level of attainment of the learning goals as specified in the IEP. The targets on which grades are based are clear to all parties. The teacher understands various measures of central tendency (average, median, mode) and understands when each is the most appropriate one to use to accurately describe student achievement.

Rubric for Evaluating Grading Practices *(continued)*

Criterion	Beginning	Developing	Fluent
6. Verifying assessment quality	There is little evidence of consideration of the accuracy/quality of the individual assessments on which grades are based. Quality standards for classroom assessment are not considered and the teacher has trouble articulating standards for quality. Assessments are rarely modified for special needs students when such modifications would provide much more accurate information about student learning.	The teacher tries to base grades on accurate assessment results only, but may not consciously understand all the features of a sound assessment. Some standards of quality are adhered to in judging the accuracy of the assessment results on which grades are based. The teacher can articulate some of these standards; or, uses standards for quality assessment intuitively, but has trouble articulating why an assessment is sound. Assessments are modified for special needs students, but the procedures used may not result in accurate information and/or match provisions in the IEP.	Grades are based only on accurate assessment results. Questionable results are not included. The teacher can articulate standards of quality, and can show evidence of consideration of these standards in classroom assessments: ■ clear and appropriate learning targets ■ clear and appropriate users and uses ■ choosing the best assessment method ■ writing clear, unambiguous questions ■ good sampling ■ avoiding potential sources of bias and mismeasurement) Assessments are modified for special needs students in ways that match instructional modifications described in IEPs. Such modifications result in generating accurate information on student achievement.
7. Involving students	Grades are a surprise to students because (1) students don't understand the basis on which they are determined, (2) students have not been involved in their own assessment (learning targets are not clear to them, and/or they do not self-assess and track progress toward the targets); or (3) teacher feedback is only evaluative (a judgment of level of quality) and includes no descriptive component.	Grades are somewhat of a surprise to students because student-involvement practices and descriptive feedback are too limited to give them insights into the nature of the learning targets being pursued and their own performance.	Grades are not a surprise to students because (a) students understand the basis for the grades received, (2) students have been involved in their own assessment (they understand the learning targets they are to hit, self-assess in relation to the targets, track their own progress toward the targets, and/or talk about their progress), and/or (3) teacher communication to students is frequent, descriptive, and focuses on what they have learned as well as the next steps in learning. Descriptive feedback is related directly to specific and clear learning targets.

Source: From *Classroom Assessment for Student Learning: Doing It Right—Using It Well* (pp. 328–330) by R. J. Stiggins, J. A. Arter, J. Chappuis, and S. Chappuis, 2004, Portland, OR: Assessment Training Institute. Copyright © 2010, 2006, 2004 by Pearson. Reprinted by permission of Pearson.

Appendix B
Survey on Marking and Grading Practices

Instructions

There are three parts to the survey. The first part asks about your current grading practices. The second part asks your opinions about grading. The third part asks about your confidence in various areas. Taking this survey at the beginning and the end of study on grading can be a useful way to track and digest changes in your thinking and practices.

Definitions

Marking is the process of providing an evaluative judgment on a single piece of work. In the United States this is called grading individual pieces of work.

Grading is the process of summarizing marks over a period of time for external reporting.

Part 1 Current Grading Practices

	Almost Always	Frequently	Sometimes	Never
1. I include one or more of the following in grades: effort, participation, tardiness, attendance, and/or adherence to class rules.				
2. I reduce points/marks on work submitted late.				
3. I give bonus points for extra credit.				
4. I reduce marks/grades for cheating.				
5. I organize information in my record/marking/gradebook by source: homework, quizzes, tests, labs, etc.				
6. I include in grades zeros for missing work.				
7. I communicate feedback on assessments by providing a single letter grade)				
8. I provide detailed comments to students about strengths and weaknesses in their work.				

9. I include performance on homework into final grades.				
10. I keep separate track of information from formative and summative assessments.				
11. I allow students to redo assessments without penalty if they have not done well. (NBPTS study)				
12. I allow new evidence to replace, not simply be added to old evidence.				
13. My students understand how grades will be calculated and what evidence will count.				

Part 2 Opinions About Grading

	Agree	Somewhat Agree	Somewhat Disagree	Disagree
14. The ONLY purpose for grades/marks should be to communicate student learning as of a point in time.				
15. One should NEVER include group scores in grades for individual students.				
15. There should be a limit to the number of students who receive marks/grades of A.				
17. Assessments and marks/grades should demonstrate how well students are doing relative to one another.				
18. It is most accurate to base grades on the mean (average) score rather than the median (middle) or mode (most frequent) score.				
19. Peer and self-assessment should be limited to formative assessment because only teachers should assign grades/marks.				

Part 3 Confidences

	Very Confident	Somewhat Confident	A Little Confident
20. I can design or find assessments that provide an accurate picture of student learning on particular learning targets/objectives.			
21. I can prepare assessment plans for units that show when formative and summative assessments will occur and how they interact.			
22. I can assign grades that support learning.			

References

Archbishop Macdonald High School. 2006. *2006–2007 Student handbook.* Edmonton, AB: Author.

Arter, J. A., & J. Chappuis. 2006. *Creating and recognizing quality rubrics.* Portland, OR: Pearson Assessment Training Institute.

Bailey, J., & J. McTighe. 1996. Reporting achievement at the secondary school level: What and how? In T. R. Guskey (Ed.), *Communicating student learning: The ASCD yearbook 1996* (pp. 119–140), Alexandria, VA: ASCD.

Benevino, M., & D. Snodgrass. 1998. *Collaborative learning in middle and secondary schools: Applications and assessments.* Larchmont, NY: Eye on Education.

Black, P., & D. Wiliam. 1998. Inside the black box: Raising standards through classroom assessment. *Phi Delta Kappan, 80*(2): 139–148.

Bondy, E., & D. D. Ross. 2008. The teacher as warm demander. *Educational* Leadership, 66(1), 54–58.

Brookhart, S. 2004. *Grading.* Upper Saddle River, NJ: Merrill/Prentice Hall.

Burkett, E. 2002. *Another planet: A year in the life of a suburban high school.* New York: Perennial.

Butler S.M., & N. D. McMunn. 2006. *A teacher's guide to classroom assessment: Understanding and using classroom assessment to improve student learning.* San Francisco: Jossey-Bass.

Carr, J. 2000. Technical issues of grading methods. In E. Trumbull & B. Farr (Eds.), *Grading and reporting in an age of standards* (pp. 45–70). Norwood, MA: Christopher Gordon.

Chappuis, J. 2009. *Seven strategies of assessment* for *learning.* Portland, OR: Pearson Assessment Training Institute.

Chappuis, S., & R. J. Stiggins. 2002. Classroom assessment for learning. *Educational Leadership, 60*(1), 40–43.

Cizek, G. J. 2003. *Detecting and preventing classroom cheating: Promoting integrity in assessment.* Thousand Oaks, CA: Corwin.

Clements, A. 2004. *The report card.* New York: Simon & Schuster.

Cooper, D. 2007. *Talk about assessment.* Toronto, ON: Nelson Education.

Cooper, D. 2010. *Talk about assessment: High school strategies and tools.* Toronto, ON: Nelson Education.

Costa, A. 1991. *Developing minds: A resource book for teaching thinking.* Alexandria, VA: ASCD.

Covington, M., & K. Manheim Teel. 1996. *Overcoming student failure: Changing motives and incentives for learning.* Washington, DC: American Psychological Association.

Darling-Hammond, L. 2010. *Performance counts: Assessment systems that support high-quality learning.* Washington, DC: Council of Chief State School Officers.

Davies, A. 2000. *Making classroom assessment work.* Merville, BC: Classroom Connections.

Deddeh, H., E. Main, & S. Ratzlaff Fulkerson. 2010. Eight steps to meaningful grading. *Phi Delta Kappan, 91*(7), 53–58.

DuFour, R., R. Eaker, R. DuFour, & G. Karhanek. 2004. *Whatever it takes: How professional learning communities respond when kids don't learn.* Bloomington, IN: Solution Tree.

Dyck, B. A. 2002. Student-led conferences up close and personal. *Middle Ground,* 6(2) 39–41.

Gardner, H. 2002. Testing for aptitude, not for speed. *New York Times,* 18, July, n.p.

Gathercoal, F. 2004. *Judicious discipline* (6th ed., rev.). San Francisco: Caddo Gap.

Gibbs, J. 2000. *A new way of learning and being together.* Windsor, ON: CenterSource Systems.

Ginsberg, M. 2004. *Motivation matters: A workbook for school change.* San Francisco: Jossey-Bass.

Guskey, T. R. (Ed.). 1996a. *Communicating student learning: The ASCD yearbook 1996.* Alexandria, VA: ASCD.

Guskey, T. R. 1996b. Reporting on student learning: Lessons from the past—prescriptions for the future. In T. R. Guskey (Ed.), *Communicating student learning: The ASCD yearbook 1996* (pp. 13–24). Alexandria, VA: ASCD.

Guskey, T. R. 2002. Computerized gradebooks and the myth of objectivity. *Phi Delta Kappan, 83*(10), 777–778.

Guskey, T. R. 2004. The communication challenge of standards-based reporting. *Phi Delta Kappan, 86*(4), 326–329.

Guskey, T. R. 2005. Zero alternatives. *Principal Leadership, 5*(2): 49–53.

Guskey, T. R., & J. Bailey. 2001. *Developing grading and reporting systems for student learning.* Thousand Oaks, CA: Corwin.

Guskey, T. R., & J. Bailey. 2010. *Developing standards-based report cards.* Thousand Oaks, CA: Corwin.

Helderman, R. S. 2004, 21 June. Thrown for a loss by SOL's. *Washington Post,* p. B01.

Johnson, D. W., & R. T. Johnson. 2004. *Assessing students in groups; Promoting group responsibility and individual accountability.* Thousand Oaks, CA: Corwin.

Kagan, S. 1995. Group grades miss the mark. *Educational Leadership, 52*(8): 68–71.

Kendall, J., & R. J. Marzano. 1997. *Content knowledge: A compendium of standards and benchmarks for K–12 education.* Aurora, CO: McREL.

Kohn, A. 1993. *Punished by rewards: The trouble with gold stars, incentive plans, A's, praise and other bribes.* New York: Houghton Mifflin.

Manitoba Education and Training. 1997. *Reporting on student progress and achievement: A policy handbook for teachers, administrators and parents.* Winnipeg, MN: Author.

Manitoba Education, Citizenship and Youth. 2006. *Policies and procedures for standards tests, 2006–2007.* Winnipeg, MB: Author.

Marshall, M. 2001a. *Discipline without stress.* Los Alamitos, CA: Piper.

Marshall, M. 2001b. *Promoting Responsibility Newsletter,* 1(4).

Marzano, R. J. 2000. *Transforming classroom grading.* Alexandria, VA: ASCD.

Marzano, R. J., & J. Kendall. 1996. *A comprehensive guide to developing standards-based districts, schools, and classrooms.* Aurora, CO: McREL.

McMann, G. 2003, 15 October. Letter to the editor. *Toronto* [ON] *Globe and Mail,* n.p.

McTighe, J. 1996–1997. What happens between assessments. *Educational Leadership, 54*(4): 6–12.

McTighe, J., & K. O'Connor. 2005. Seven practices for effective learning. *Educational Leadership, 63*(3), 10–17.

Montgomery County Public Schools. n.d. *Framework for improving teaching and learning.* Rockville, MD: Author. Available at www.mcps.k12.md.us/ departments/dsd/leadership/handouts/ lookfors.pdf.

O'Connor, K. 1995. Guidelines for grading that support learning and student success. *NASSP Bulletin, 79*(5), 91–95.

O'Connor, K. 1999. *The mindful school: How to grade for learning.* Arlington Heights, IL: Skylight.

O'Connor, K. 2001. The principal's role in report card grading. *NASSP Bulletin, 85* (625): 37–46.

O'Connor, K. 2002. *How to grade for learning: Linking grades to standards* (2d ed.). Thousand Oaks, CA: Corwin.

O'Connor, K. 2009. *How to grade for learning: Linking grades to standards* (3rd ed.). Thousand Oaks, CA: Corwin.

Patterson, W. 2003. Breaking out of our boxes. *Phi Delta Kappan, 84*(8): 569–574.

Phi Delta Kappa International. 2010. The pathway to high performance. *Edge, 5*(5): 3–18.

Pink, D. 2009. *Drive: The surprising truth about what motivates us.* New York: Riverhead.

Reeves, D. B. 2000. Standards are not enough: Essential transformations for school success. *NASSP Bulletin, 84*(620): 5–19.

Reeves, D. B. 2004. The case against the zero. *Phi Delta Kappan, 86*(4), 324–325.

Reeves, D. B. 2006. *The learning leader: How to focus school improvement for better results.* Alexandria, VA: ASCD.

Rogers, S., J. Ludington, & S. Graham. 1998. *Motivation and learning.* Evergreen, CO: Peak Learning Systems.

School District of Clayton, MO. 2003. *2003 Annual report.* Clayton, MO: Author.

SmartBrief. 2001, 19 December. Alexandria, VA: ASCD.

Standards for foreign language learning. n.d. Yonkers, NY: American Council on the Teaching of Foreign Languages. Available at www.yearoflanguages .org/files/public/execsumm.pdf.

Starsinic, J. 2003, 21 November. Letter to the editor. *Harrisburg* (PA) *Patriot News,* n.p.

Stiggins, R. J. 2001. *Student-involved classroom assessment,* 3rd ed. Upper Saddle River, NJ: Merrill/Prentice Hall.

Stiggins, R. J. 2005. *Student-involved assessment* for *learning,* 4th ed. Upper Saddle River, NJ: Merrill/Prentice Hall.

Stiggins. R. J., J. A. Arter, J. Chappuis, & S. Chappuis. 2004. *Classroom assessment* for *student learning: Doing it right—using it well.* Portland, OR: Pearson Assessment Training Institute.

Stiggins, R. J., & J. Chappuis. 2005. Using student-involved classroom assessment to close achievement gaps. *Theory into Practice, 44*(1), 11–18.

Szatanski, B., & C. Taafe. 1999. *Classrooms of choice: A teacher's guide to creating the dynamic classroom.* Ottawa, ON: Cebra.

Tombari, M., & G. Borich. 1999. *Authentic assessment in the classroom.* Upper Saddle River, NJ: Merrill/Prentice Hall.

Tomlinson, C. A., & J. McTighe. 2006. *Integrating differentiated instruction and understanding by design.* Alexandria, VA: ASCD.

Toronto (ON) *National Post.* 2001, 18 April. Title unavailable. p. F3.

Webber C. F., N. Aitken, J. Lupart, & S. Scott. 2009. *The Alberta student assessment study: Final report.* Edmonton, Alberta: Government of Alberta—Education. Retrieved March 23, 2010 from http:// education.alberta.ca/media/1165612/ albertaassessmentstudyfinalreport.pdf.

Wiggins, G. 2000. Posted comment. Retrieved 19 January 2000 from www. chatserver.ascd.org.

Wiliam, D. 2003. Assessment and learning. Presentation to ATL Summer Conference, London, UK. June.

Wormeli, R. 2006. *Fair isn't always equal: Assessing and grading in the differentiated classroom.* Portland, ME: Stenhouse.

Wright, R. 1994. Success for all: The median is the key. *Phi Delta Kappan, 75*(9), 723–725.

zhengfranklin. 2008. Excerpt from blog in response to "At Thomas Jefferson, 2.8 Is Tantamount to Failure." Washingtonpost.com, July 27. Accessed at www.washingtonpost .com/wp-dyn/content/article/ 2008/07/25/AR2008072503104_ Comments.html#

Index